W9-APR-227

Agris

Sambahan Inn

Temple

Temple

Sambahan

Temple

Rai Pasti

Roda

Lecuk

Temple

Arjana

Siti-Bungalows

Temple

Temple

Puri-
Lukisan-
Museum

Hotel Ubud

Taman

Andong

Pum Kantor

Suci Inn

awar

Mumbul

Saraswati

Puri
Saren
Agung

Kutuh

Police

ya

Menara

Temple

Puri Pusaka

Pondok-
Indah

Suarsena

Temple

a

Bina Wisata
Information

Market

Mustika

Brati

Suarsana

Tjanderi

Yuni's

Sutresna

Ubud Raya

Temple

Okawati

Alit's

Hbiscus

Wena

Dana

Griva Taman
Sari

Gerudug

stache

Puri-Muwa

Dewa

Gayatri

Shana

Tantri

Bamboo Garden

Pharmacy

Lastri

Badra

Nirvana
Agung

Post Office

Temple

Sari-
Nadi

Igna

Ibu Rai

Yoga

Ad

Igna

Bendi

Suartha

Nick's

Warji

Dian

Rama Sita

Ibu Masih

Ambengan

Kerta

Clinic

Temple

Indra

Temple

Weda

Temple

Gerhana Sari

Frog Pond

Owi Ari

Tebesaya

Rice Mill

Jati

Budi

Pande

Mendra
s

Nani's

Temple

Jaya

Warsa

Padangtegal

Temple

Peliatan

Sagitarius

Temple

Fibra

Artini

Ubud Inn

Mandala Bungalows

Monkey Forest Pension

Temple

Mandala Homestay

Mudita

Rice Mill

Detri

Puri Agung

Banyan Tree

Kubuku

Ibu Arsa

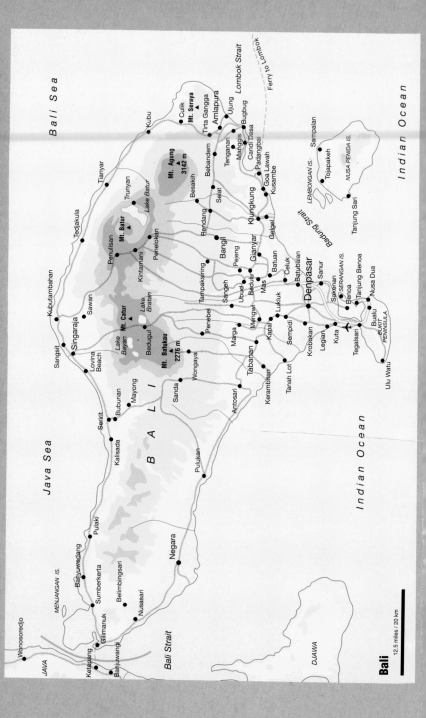

Bali

12.5 miles / 20 km

BALI
Bird Walks

Written and Presented by **Victor Mason**

INSIGHT
pocket
GUIDES

Insight Pocket Guide:

 Bird Walks

Directed by
Hans Höfer

Managing Editor
Francis Dorai

Photography by
Ingo Jezierski

Design Concept by
V. Barl

Design by
Karen Hoisington

© **1994 APA Publications (HK) Ltd**

All Rights Reserved

Printed in Singapore by
Höfer Press (Pte) Ltd
Fax: 65-8616438

Distributed in the United States by
Houghton Mifflin Company
222 Berkeley Street
Boston, Massachusetts 02116-3764
ISBN: 0-395-69014-5

Distributed in Canada by
Thomas Allen & Son
390 Steelcase Road East
Markham, Ontario L3R 1G2
ISBN: 0-395-69014-5

Distributed in the UK & Ireland by
GeoCenter International UK Ltd
The Viables Center, Harrow Way
Basingstoke, Hampshire RG22 4BJ
ISBN: 9-62421-531-6

Worldwide distribution enquiries:
Höfer Communications Pte Ltd
38 Joo Koon Road
Singapore 2262
ISBN: 9-62421-531-6

NO part of this book may be reproduced,
stored in a retrieval system or transmitted in any form
or means electronic, mechanical, photocopying,
recording or otherwise, without prior written
permission of Apa Publications. Brief text quotations
with use of photographs are exempted for book review
purposes only.
As every effort is made to provide accurate information
in this publication, we would appreciate it if readers
would call our attention to any errors that may occur by
communicating with Apa Villa, 81 The Cut, London
SE1 8LL. Tel: 71-620-0008, Fax: 71-620-1074.
Information has been obtained from sources believed
to be reliable, but its accuracy and completeness,
and the opinions based thereon, are not guaranteed.

Selamat Datang!

Victor Mason

As a keen walker and bird-watcher, I must have tramped every cart-and-goat track within an 8-km (5-mile) radius of Ubud a hundred times or more. Despite this, the path is still full of surprises, with each bend in the trail bringing some new revelation.

This book is essentially an introduction to the Balinese countryside, the habitat of our birds and other wild creatures. Nearly all the trails are circular, starting and ending at the bridge in Campuhan, Ubud, in the heart of Bali where there is superb walking and running country. Some are tougher than others and are graded accordingly: one foot (🦶) denotes an easy stroll or ramble, two feet (🦶🦶) a bit of a scramble and three feet (🦶🦶🦶) a fairly hard slog. Things you may need, such as bathers for a swim, sarongs for women entering temples, or a packed lunch, are indicated at the beginning of each itinerary. Most of the itineraries earn a two feet rating or more and none are tricky or dangerous.

There are two seasons — wet and dry — but no intense monsoonal rain or drought. The best time to visit corresponds with the Austral winter, the south-easterly trades prevailing through the coolest months from May to August. I can think of nowhere more agreeable — physically, ethnically, climatically — in any sense. Proof of this is the fact that I have made my home here for more than 20 years, running the Beggars' Bush Restaurant above Campuhan Bridge, and starting the Bali Bird Club.

Being *in situ* at the sign of the Beggars' Bush (which is home of the Hash House Harriers and the Bali Bird Club), I shall always be delighted to meet seekers of the real Bali and to point them in the right direction. *Selamat Datang* — Welcome!

Contents

Preamble

Worldly paradise: They say that Bali is one of the most beautiful places on earth. That 'the Morning of the World' is indeed a worldly paradise, or as the Balinese themselves believe, a terrestrial replica of that other realm which is the garden of Indra, Lord of Heaven, and where the eternal soul may rest in grace awaiting transmigration. And of course, they are right: both they, the visitors and the Balinese, that race of inheritants which is truly blessed.

'Hello turis!': Visitors to this enchanted isle – or, more accurately, tourists – are constantly hailed by a host of brown, beaming faces and voices straining in urgent chorus: 'Turis! Turis!' It is a perfectly correct as well as practical appellation; for the Balinese are nothing if not practical.

On foot: Since from the start we are to be branded 'tourists' irrespective of our motives, activities, or cherished pursuits, we may as well make the most of it. We should be firmly determined to be the best tourists that ever set foot in the place. And that is the key. For, undeniably, the best way to explore and discover a new country is on foot. There is absolutely no substitute for feet!

To the pedestrian, no plain or forest, grotto, scarp or mountaintop is inaccessible. Given time and inclination, and a pair of fairly sturdy legs, the horizon, if not literally the sky, may be said to be the limit.

Four-wheeled vehicles: There was a time when I would have recommended the use of a motorcycle as the most effective means of covering great distances and journeying from base to a selected point at which to dismount and walk.

With the tremendous increase in road traffic during recent years, and the alarming incidence of serious accidents involving motorcycles in collision with trucks and buses, allied with the lack of medical facilities in local hospitals, I can only counsel one to stick to four-wheeled vehicles at all times.

Bicycles, if carefully serviced and properly managed, are all right up to a point and over short distances. But one must always be ready to yield all available road space to faster and heavier machines, sometimes with disastrous consequences. Besides, it should be remembered that Bali is nearly all up or down, which implies that, for the most part, 'push-bikes' are well described as such.

Far better, assuming there no restrictions on time, to walk everywhere always. And where time is of the essence, best to hire a motorcar, or rely exclusively on public transport.

Bemo or colt: As in other so-called Third World countries, the public road transport system in Indonesia is simply superb. There are neither scheduled stops nor timetables. At any hour of the day (and even night on main arterial highways), all you have to do is stand by the wayside and wait. Before very long, a bus or lesser conveyance – notably *Bemo* (small covered pick-up truck) or *Colt* (minibus) – will come tearing along and, with a great shrieking of brakes and swirling of smoke and dust, shudder to a halt at your very elbow. To signal it to stop at all is plainly less necessary than it is to get out of the thing's way.

These convenient vehicles ply set routes and will stop at a moment's notice to pick up and disgorge passengers anywhere along the way. It is possible to charter them for a substantial consideration and proceed in other directions. Travelling considerable distances may involve several stops and changes, but will not inflict long intervals of considerable discomfort.

Orang biasa: Standard fares are very low, but, inevitably, the *orang turis* is requested and expected to pay extra. The trick is of course to feign omniscience, say nothing, and tender no more nor less than the amount exacted from the regular rank and file, *orang biasa*.

Trudging on blacktop: In following the itineraries in this book, it may be assumed that the beginnings of all trails are accessible by some means of public conveyance. In any case, the aim throughout is to avoid unnecessary trudging on blacktop roads. I never cease to be astonished by the spectacle of ever more populous bands of joggers – let alone hikers! – pounding their weary way along the shoulders and verges of busy paved roads when there is such abundance of unscarred countryside to run through. It is not only extremely tedious but literally dicing with death – instant on impact or insidiously slow through the inhalation of exhaust fumes.

Students on a school outing: Speaking of pollution, I feel it is entirely appropriate to put in here a special plea to preserve the unsullied beauty of our landscape. It is a sad fact that many picnickers and hikers do leave an appalling mess behind them, and I have to say, at the risk of causing some indignation, that it is mainly locals who are at fault. Not just students on a school outing, or field workers, or household ladies laundering in the creek, but rather shopkeepers and restaurant owners who tend to dispose of all their refuse in the nearest stream or ditch.

Discarded plastic: Yet who can say that they are wholly to blame? In the past few years the problem has been exacerbated by the introduction of plastic packaged mineral water. No matter where one walks, every dike and drain and ditch is choked with discarded plastic water bottles. When the rains come, all the watercourses are awash with them. The affronted ocean throws up its unwanted quota to augment the piles of rotting rubbish on the beach.

Plantain and palm-leaf: I remember when, apart from aerated waters and perishable provisions packed in ceramic, glass or metal, the only wrapping material employed in local stores was plantain and palm-leaf. Whatever was thrown away was, in the current jargon, biodegradable, whilst more durable containers such as glass bottles were retained for further use or put out for collection by the neighbourhood rag-and-bone merchant.

Meanwhile, if you must take a container of any kind in your ruck-sack, please, whatever you do, do not toss it away when you have emptied it.

Travelling light: Is it really necessary to encumber oneself with bottles of water or beer or, indeed, with anything at all? It is not exactly as if one has to negotiate immense uncharted wastes, or struggle *in extremis* over endless desert dunes. Being a great believer in travelling light, I never carry anything more than a pair of binoc-ulars, pencil and notebook, and a modest sum of money in my pocket.

Perennial springs: Should refreshment be required, there are always the wayside stalls, *warung*, where delicious tea or cof-fee may be had, and an assortment of rather villainous-looking soft drinks.

In some areas, notably around Pejeng and Karangasem, the most excellent palm toddy, locally called *tuak*, and its distil-late, *arak*, may be obtained. And every village has its mobile stand of jars containing drinks of solid, lurid colour, concocted from var-ious leaves, seaweed, sago, tapioca, etc., which are extremely good and nourishing.

Throughout the hilly regions, wherever ravines and valleys have been formed, perennial springs gush forth their crystalline sweetness. This sparkling product of filtration by a billion tons of pumice is immeasurably brighter and purer than anything that comes in a bottle.

To locate the source, simply ask for *air* (pronounced ire) *minum*, which is drinking water, or *pantjoran* (waterspout), or retrace the steps of village maidens with buckets poised upon their heads. Often set in spectacular surrounds and associated with beautifully-wrought river temples, *pura beji*, such watering-places are always worth a visit, whether one is thirsty and hot, or not.

Bare minimum: Equipment and clothing too should be kept to a bare minimum: the tendency is to take far more than is required. I never carry a change of clothes with me, or wear anything more than a pair of shorts and a shirt. These may be washed and aired and dried in no time at all, if such is really necessary. For women, a *sarong* (length of cotton usually of batik print) is an all-purpose garment for swimwear, towelling or modest cover-up over shorts when entering a temple.

13

Bother with boots: Nor do I bother with boots which only serve to give your feet blisters, and cause them to sweat and smell. Only in very dry, rocky terrain or for the purpose of scaling volcanic slopes littered with debris, do I advocate some form of footwear. And, unless one is compelled to stray from the trail in quest of edible fungi or some *rara avis*, I would advise against socks and shoes in the jungle. For, if there are leeches, remove them before they attach themselves. But, obviously, I do not recommend to all who habitually wear shoes that they should henceforth go unshod. It takes time for the feet to harden and protective callouses to form.

Tread carefully: Whether shod or unshod, I do, however, urge you to tread carefully in a metaphorical way. Proceed cautiously with respect not only to terrain, but to the environment, and to the social customs and sensibilities of those who inhabit it. Despite the vast influx of visitors, who tend moreover to be gregarious and stay within well defined boundaries, there still exist a number of places where visitors have yet to penetrate, and where the intrusion of a foreigner can have an awesome effect.

Realm of faerie: The slightest deviation from well-trodden track transports the wayfarer to the realm of faerie or Middle Earth, where nothing much has changed in centuries. Often have I entered into that other world a bit briskly and incautiously, only to trigger off a fearful round of livestock stampeding, dogs howling, and bewildered children rushing, shrieking, for their mothers.

On several occasions have I had reports of stones and other missiles being hurled at visitors venturing into remoter parts. Such unpleasant outbursts were nine times out of ten, I am convinced, kindled not so much by malice as by sheer terror – the child's pristine terror of the bogey-man. I am convinced because it has happened to me!

Tree-ants: Physical obstacles and noxious objects to be encountered along the way are mercifully few. For a country situated so signally within the tropics, the overall dearth of poisonous species and frightful creepy-crawlies is remarkable. Things to watch out for, besides clinging leeches which are found only in damp forest undergrowth, are the vicious, stinging red tree-ants.

Inflicted en masse, their bite is quite painful: sinking their mandibles into your flesh, they are absolute brutes to dislodge, as I have often found to my discomfort. Beware of walking in the proximity of freshly-felled trees which harbour the ants' disturbed nests; for in an instant furious swarms rush up your legs – another cogent argument for not wearing trousers!

Another kind of ant, also red but much smaller, patchily frequents the bunds of flooded paddyfields. Known as *smut api*, fire ants, and with a similar propensity to swarm rapidly, these little demons pack a sensationally lingering sting, which has the searing intensity of hundreds of red-hot needles.

Tiger's claws: It is in the floral department that the most malevolent perils lurk. First in pricking order is the coral-bean or tiger's claws tree, known by the Balinese name *tjangin*, which is a kind of *Erythrina*. The scarlet flowers which grow in clusters and resemble claws in shape are very attractive to insects and birds, as well as to the human eye, but there the attraction ends. For the entire tree is covered with spines – in some species even the leaves – which are not only needle-sharp but also toxic to the touch.

Tjangin trees are often planted in rows bordering irrigation canals, and the farmers employ their thorny branches in erecting fences or barriers across paddy bunds and pathways – a most effective deterrent to passage!

To step on the spiny limbs is excruciatingly painful – much like stepping on a sea-urchin – and the thorns are quite capable of piercing rubber soles. On numerous occasions have I inadvertently caught hold of a coral-bean stem whilst trying to steady myself on a steep river bank or other slope, with agonising consequences.

Malu-malu: Then there is a type of creeping *mimosa* (**M. pudica**), adorned with purple flowering pompoms, commonly called the sensitive plant on account of the curious tendency of its leaves to fold tightly at the slightest touch. Hence, the locally given name *malu-malu*, meaning retiring or shy.

Found mainly on level wasteland and grassy areas, this deceptively delicate plant of such pleasing appearance bears rows of tenacious prickles which puncture and slash, similar to brambles in a temperate clime.

Worst of all is a kind of stinging nettle found at higher elevations. It is particularly rife in the Bedugul region, being notable for its large, heart-shaped leaves, generally of rather ragged appearance due to the depredations of caterpillars, and covered with silky white hairs. Brushing against these is akin to being badly singed or scalded, producing livid welts on the skin, and residual inflammation which endures for days, if not weeks. Thus it is advisable not to stray from well-marked forest trails.

Innumerable ravines: I mentioned physical obstacles. Besides fences made of the *tjangin* tree, what impede progress through the countryside are the innumerable ravines, formed by the rapid erosion of stream beds composed of volcanic tuff.

Such obstruction is all the more apparent when travelling from east to west in the path of the sun. In fact, it can be extremely difficult as well as dangerous to proceed any distance in a poor light. What seems to be level ground all the way to a horizon of shimmering palms enfolding a sleepy hamlet is dissected by not one but several chasms of varying depth and declivity. You come suddenly upon them, gaping, gurgling and treacherous, and realise that an impasse has been reached.

Inevitably one's search is finally rewarded by the sight of rough steps hewn from the rock face, descending to a teetering bamboo bridge or down to the rushing water itself. Some of these passages, while readily negotiable by Balinese men and women bearing huge loads, may be steep and perilous, and cannot be recommended to the casual visitor out for an evening stroll. Far better to retrace your steps, or continue on to the nearest main village thoroughfare or road where a proper bridge exists.

Snakes: Finally, allow me to disillusion you on the subject of snakes. These much maligned and miserably persecuted creatures are abundant in Bali, though you will seldom see them on any main path, for the poor things, being ultra-sensitive to the earth's vibration, are rudely disturbed and slither quickly out of harm's way long before you erupt noisily on the scene.

While there are poisonous cobras and pit-vipers here, the vast majority is harmless. Seriously, have you ever been bitten by a snake? Have you ever come across anyone who has been bitten by a snake? Do you know anyone who knows anyone who ...?

At the same time, one must allow that a very real fear of snakes, technically known as ophidiaphobia, does possess some people; but I think the symptoms are more likely to manifest themselves in a confined space such as a bathroom than in the open air.

Snakes, besides being rather beautiful animals, also keep down the rat population, and the household that sensibly lodges king cobras in its roof will soon be rodent-free. If, in the course of your wanderings, you are ever confronted by one, which is only likely to occur when the snake is unlucky enough to find itself cornered, then kindly move out of its way, permitting it free passage. Never, in any circumstances, should you attempt to kill a snake. Discourage small children from playing with them, especially should they be short and black, or long and bright green!

Stunning profusion: What else may we expect to discover during our cross-country peregrinations? If we have eyes to see, we may be well rewarded in the select fields of ornithology, entomology and botany – birds, butterflies and other insects, and plants with special reference to flowers and trees.

When by their outstanding beauty or peculiarity these should merit attention, I shall point them out along the way. Great panoramas, ancient monuments, and strategic watering-holes too, whenever these compel us to pause and admire the paradisiacal productions on offer. For Bali has them all in stunning profusion.

Things change: Even as I write, things change. Not only with the construction of new buildings and new roads where formerly there was none, but also with encroaching cultivation and the despoliation of every patch of unkempt ground where Nature has been allowed to take her course. Marginal land development to meet the needs of expanding population is understandable, as is the necessity of clearing and foraging in the odd overgrown hollow for firewood and fodder. But some village cemeteries are also being singled out for tidying up, possibly with a view to gaining points in the regional competition for best-ordered community.

All of which is a pity, for soon there will be no suitable cover for the birds to nest in (if they have not all been shot), and no tangled vines for caterpillars to feed on. And no more mysterious dark corners for us to chance upon and wonderingly penetrate.

As waterways will dry up and alter course, so will beaten paths, cease to be frequented, become overgrown and vanish, only to pop up anew a few paces further on. A fallen tree or landslip may cause as great a deviation as the building of a highway or erection of a bridge.

Someone will come: So, if the odd trail seems unfamiliar and landmark strangely altered or altogether non-existent, bear with me, and, assuming some sense of direction, persist. If possible, set your sights on some outstanding feature of the local topography, or at least align yourself with the sun, and, if needs be, the stars.

If the worst comes to the worst, I can tell you that it is not easy to lose one's way in Bali; and though a wrong turn may be taken, it is well nigh impossible to become irretrievably lost. No matter where one finds oneself, by day or by night, seemingly stranded in the wilderness, ankle twisted, wheel punctured, second winded, out of gas – no matter where ... someone will come. Someone will pop out from behind that bush, and, having ministered unto you, point you in the right direction.

Right, Pura Desa Singakerta

The Bridge.

Standing on the bridge at **Campuhan**, peering down into the cool, green under-storey and dappled recesses of the ravine, at once the melting bitumen embedded in concrete reality slips away. With it, the tumult of traffic, and all vocal and mechanical articulation.

The stream, now clear and rushing, brawls among islands of soft rock eroded from sheer, green-clad cliffs. Turbid and swirling, it sweeps over and onwards, washing the westerly wall of **Ubud** with its alluvial flood, bearing away the effluent of new housing estates. In its downward flight, it replenishes a mosaic of cultivated terraces and water-courses before debouching, fulfilled yet depleted, on the

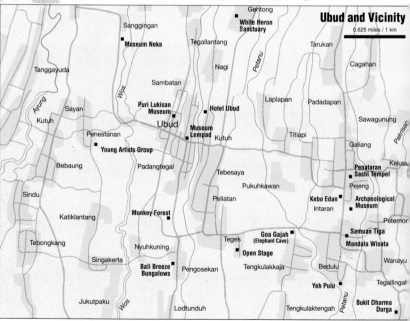

Ubud and Vicinity
0.625 miles / 1 km

Bridge at Campuhan

coast south of **Sukawati**.

Not wholly depleted. A comingling of numerous spring-fed tributaries tumbling in impenetrable gorges, the **Wos** (for that is the name of the river in Campuhan) is as untameable as it is unpredictable. The huge boulders and collapsed masonry of underground irrigation tunnels, concreted weirs and piers of former bridges littering its bed will testify to this.

Unlike its more spectacular neighbour, the mighty **Ayung**, thundering through scenic canyons in the central uplands and over the barrages at **Kedewatan** and **Mambal**, whence the main flow is diverted to water all the land of **Badung Regency**, the capricious Wos runs unimpeded to the coastal plain. As the builders of the mainroad bridge south of Sukawati discovered at their third attempt to span the river in unseasonable spate, the precast concrete piers were no match for the force of the flood unleashed against them.

Today, as on any other day, it is sunny and mild, and the translucent water sparkles and invites us to bathe in the cool, fresh current that gently massages and soothes the overstretched and heated frame. Already, lissome brown forms disport directly below, bobbing about in the eddies and races formed where the two streams become one.

At this important confluence from which the local hamlet takes its name – Campuhan being a variant of *campuran*, meaning a mixture or blending of elements – at this propitious meeting of the life-giving waters, stands the sacred enclave upon the shoulder moulded by the two tributaries

Wos river from Campuhan bridge

Barong dance

of the Wos.

It was here, not long after the dissolution of the **Madjapahit Empire** at the end of the 15th century, that the great Brahmanic divine, *Pedanda* **Wawu Rauh**, whose name is known to every Balinese grown-up and child, and his disciples established that most perfect of temples, the **Pura Campuhan**. Though there is evidence that the origins may go back to the 8th century when the pioneering Buddhist followers of Sri Markandia first settled here.

To this hallowed place come pilgrims from all over Bali. Around the time of major festivals such as *Galungan* and *Kuningan* (a kind of Balinese celebration of the Feasts of All Saints and All Souls, when ancestral spirits return to earth to be received and entertained by their descendants), all the villagers for miles about throng the way to *Pura* Campuhan.

They arrive in resplendent procession, accompanied by their *barong* (fabulous lion-like monsters endowed with fantastic magical powers) and respective temple deities, to partake in a ritual ablution (*mekiis* or *melasti*) – all urged on by the mesmeric rhythm of the marching gongs.

However, all is tranquil now, and the temple, reposing in the shade of mighty mango and banyan (*beringin*) trees, would seem to invite closer inspection while the dancing waters beam and beckon us to bathe.

If we do decide to visit the temple and enter the inner precinct, then we must cleanse ourselves in the stream before changing into fresh clothing which should include a woven or batik sarong and ceremonial sash (*selendang*).

Village girl and her makeshift hat

Ablutions

❯ • Bathers • Sarong & Sash

A gentle, exploratory stroll to Pura Campuhan which should not take more than an hour, allowing time for a swim. Descend to the river via the grounds of a hotel, once the studio of artist Walter Spies. Cross boulders to the water's edge and then up the path to the temple. After inspecting the beautifully-wrought shrines and altars, there are two easy ways to reach the main road.

There are several ways of descending to the river. The simplest, involving the least scramble, is through the garden of the Hotel Campuhan. Situated 100m (109yds) north of the bridge, this gracious retreat owes its existence to the late **Tjokorda Gedé Agung Sukawati**, Prince of Ubud, who befriended the artist **Walter Spies**.

Epitaph at Hotel Campuhan

Spies came to Ubud in the 1930s and stayed at Campuhan in a studio he had constructed on the Tjokorda's land. On their return to Bali in 1933, Rose and **Miguel Covarrubias** lived here with Spies, preparing the framework for the book, *Island of Bali*; and here, Bali's most celebrated resident toiled to produce the glowing canvases so eagerly sought by museum curators and private collectors.

Going through the hotel's entrance and reception area, render the price of admission to the swimming-pool before descending the steps leading to the garden.

Now we pass under a most magnificent tree, the identity of which has forever been a mystery to me. The massive trunk and limbs are densely covered in spines – as are some species of cotton-tree (*Chlorisia* and *Bombax*) – while the heart-shaped leaves have long, slender tips, resembling those of the **Peepul** or **Bo tree**, under which **Buddha** sat in meditation for six years. And there are peculiar fat

'A most magnificent tree'

catkins like large mulberries which are present from December to April. I should be greatly obliged to anyone who can tell us what kind of tree this is.

A little further on is the studio itself, unchanged in every respect, overlooking the swimming-pool Spies had built, I understand, at the instance of Barbara Hutton, the Woolworth heiress. On the wall adjacent to the house is inscribed an epitaph, poignant in its economy, to the memory of the man who was Bali's best-loved expatriate.

Down the next flight of steps, past the pool and skirting the wall of the tennis court, the path leads over embedded boulders to the water's edge. From time to time, a bridge fashioned from bamboo is erected for the benefit of hotel guests, only to be swept away at each seasonal flood.

Today we wade, and divesting ourselves of our dress, flop into the cooling flow and soak. A few metres downstream, at the base of a towering cliff, is a natural pool where the Balinese like to bathe. A little way upstream, in a deeper part carved out of the rock, lies a sluggish passage in which no right-minded Balinese would care to immerse himself. This is the former lair of a demon (*raksasa*) which plagued the populace, spiriting away and devouring young maidens ensnared at their devotions in temple ceremonies. The gently spinning vortex is not inviting.

On the other side of the stream the path continues up the slope, through borders of **hibiscus**, on recently installed and evenly spaced steps to emerge in a sea of coarse, long grass (*alang-alang*) behind the wall of Campuhan temple.

On the left hand it leads to a small bricked enclosure and spring under a spreading banyan which directly overlooks the hotel dearly hugging the hillside. To this spot have I seen the *barong* and his attendants brought to take the holy water. Following the path right, beneath the temple wall which looms above the eastern tributary of the stream, is a side entrance to the outer court. Here you may enter and rest on the platform of the long, tiled pavilion or *balé*, which is used for storing sheaves of *alang-*

Walter Spies' studio at Campuhan

alang, dried and ready for roofing.

Pavilion used for storing alang-alang

Now the place is deserted, but on ceremonial occasions, under these same ringing rafters, the orchestra will play. Across the way are other sheds for the preparation of offerings and the temple feast. At length, making sure that we are properly attired, we may pass through the gate to the inner courts in order to inspect the beautifully-wrought shrines and altars where offerings and prayers are rendered, and obeisances made.

Outside the split pylon of the main entrance, under a huge **mango tree**, another rough track runs abruptly down to a point just above the confluence of the streams. To return to the main road, cross over the small stone bridge, pausing to look over the parapet into the mottled race below before heading up the wide, stepped temple approach in the direction of Ubud.

Alternatively, after crossing the bridge and passing a large *beringin* concealing a crudely-cemented stone effigy of *Ganesa*, the elephant-god, bear right into the village school courtyard. Passing behind the main classroom block, climb giant steps to the roadway and emerge a few paces south of the Campuhan bridge.

Nymphs and Demons

Two separate itineraries lead to two spring-fed watering places among the most serene and resuscitating spots around Campuhan bridge. First, to consort with the nymphs at the Pantjoran Widedari (Nymph waterspout) by following Pura Campuhan approach and track which skirts Tjitjak Inn and returning the same way. Then be a bit reckless by entering a cave mouth into a black and mysterious, subterranean corridor. Second, to dispatch the demons at Pantjoran Rawana (the demon spout) by taking the road behind Antonio Blanco's gallery, bearing left to cross the Wos, then exiting via the cemetery. Both could be comfortably completed in two hours, or more with a picnic.

The term *pantjoran* denotes a waterspout or pipe from which water gushes out. *Widedari*, or *dedari*, are the heavenly nymphs of the Hindu epic *Ramayana* who dance for the pleasure of the gods.

To begin, go down the steep steps at the southern end of the bridge (opposite Murni's), and wander behind the school building

Ramayana epic in art

Kris dance

to the main temple approach. Instead of proceeding down past the *beringin* tree and over the little bridge, we should cross the rocky culvert by the steps and climb on to the concrete strip road which leads to Puri (palace) Campuhan, now the **Tjitjak Inn.** Just before the carpark, a stony, muddy path leads down following the course of the river upstream; and soon we arrive at another stone bridge, immediately before which lies the way to the spring on our right.

Going up and down some rather slippery steps, proceed along a sluice with several gushing outlets, to the cavernous recess in the cliff where the main flow tumbles from a primitively-carved stone *tugu.* The altar is surrounded by several sculpted heads – none of them noticeably ancient – including a quite impressive *barong* mask.

I can think of few pleasanter haunts for bathing: here indeed, at an unfrequented hour, might one surprise the divinities themselves attending to their toilet.

Above the spout, obscured in the darkness of the cleft, lies the cave mouth from which the spring issues forth. Should one feel adventurous – and have a certain resolution to fulfil the quest – the passage may be reached by clambering up the damp, mossy rock. Inside the dank tunnel, which is in reality an ancient man-made water conduit, it is impenetrably black and for the first part one is obliged to stoop.

Gingerly edging forward, there is the queer sensation of being fanned, if not quite brushed, by feathery – or leathery? – appendages unseen. But these are not blood-sucking vampire-bats or in fact bats of any description; they are a species of extremely common small swift, the **White-bellied Swiftlet** (*Collocalia linchi*) which chooses to nest and roost in dark caves.

A smart crack on the skull informs us that the

White-bellied
27 *swiftlet in flight*

tunnel roof is getting lower and that from now on it is necessary to crawl upstream. Before embarking on such folly, it is best to equip oneself with a flashlight as we splash on in inky blackness. But daylight is visible as we round the final curve of this sinuous passage, and press on in a position slightly less than fully erect.

Out in the open, a rough trail leads up to the ricefields (*sawa*), where, tripping along the bunds or grassy balks to the main arterial path, we follow this to a wide ramp which brings us back to the highway below the brow of the Campuhan hill. To continue to Campuhan, we pass under the aqueduct and mount the ramp on the other side of the road. The pedestrian way, situated well above the main road, is more pleasant and safer.

The second course to **Pantjoran Rawana** lies nearer at hand. The most direct access is via a narrow paved alley leading from the main road a few metres up the hill from, and on the same side as, **Murni's Warung**. The paved portion ends abruptly in a root and rubble-obstructed slope which inclines steeply between high rock walls and emerges near the spring.

I suggest that we head a few metres north of the Campuhan bridge, and take the small road directly opposite **Beggar's Bush** which brings us behind the garden wall of the studio of artist **Mario Antonio Blanco**.

To insist that we should watch our step on the way is not to overstate the case, for this tiny road bears the full flow of traffic to and from the village of **Penestanan**. An endless cavalcade of trucks hauls construction materials to the ever-increasing number of building sites which threatens to displace the terraced fields entirely. There are plans to expand and upgrade the road.

Passing behind Blanco's home, we pause to survey what remains of the cultivation ascending the ridge. For new arrivals from afar, it may be the first glimpse of the growing rice crop though there

Rice harvesting

is ample opportunity to inspect the miracle of rice production in the course of ensuing itineraries.

Today the harvest is under way, and many of the terraces are already stubbly or flooded. Flocks of ducks stand about, watchfully idle. A kingfisher, beautifully blue and purple, with an enormous scarlet bill, is perched on a plaited fence erected to contain the ducks. Quite possibly it is our first view of the **Java Kingfisher** (*Halcyon cyanoventris*) which inhabits only Java and Bali. Above us towers the dark green mantle of the banyan in Blanco's garden; and above that, vigorously pursuing the swarm of insects, mills a host of the little white-bellied swiftlets which practically brushed against us earlier in the cave.

Arriving at the junction, we turn left away from the traffic. Before turning the corner to **Sari Homestay**, we pass a gap in the hedge of hibiscus to our left. This is our opening to the little lane that runs down towards the river, behind the retaining wall of Blanco's garden. There are a couple of sidetracks to a huddle of dwellings, and a short way down on the right, there used to stand a splendid **lychee tree**. All that remains is the impressive raised root system. The paved part of the lane leads to a private house but we plunge straight down the steep and muddy steps on the track which winds out of sight into the vegetation below.

I often used to come this way to bathe in the river. But recently the enclosed passage has become rather smelly due to the fact that a disgraceful amount of rubbish

Wayang kulit puppets

Who was Rawana?

He was the demon king who, in the *Ramayana*, abducted **Sita**, the bride of **Prince Rama** and was finally slain in battle with the army of monkeys commanded by **Hanuman**. Every child is familiar with the tale, a popular episode of the shadow puppet (*wayang kulit*) screen. Rawana is Batara Kala, Lord of Darkness, who is himself a manifestation of Siwa, sent by Siwa to destroy the human race.

Remember the story of the *raksasa* who kidnapped all the young girls from *Pura* Campuhan? Invariably he would pounce on the last dancer in the line of *redjang*, a stately ceremonial temple dance performed with offerings of food and wine for the gods. On one occasion, his captive had the presence of mind to let fall a trail of blossoms from her headdress which led to the very mouth of the monster's cavern.

At length all the men of the village, together with their orchestras, assembled outside the cave where they made a great blaze and smote on the gongs, setting up such a reek and din, that the evil giant was aroused from his post-prandial slumber and stumbled blindly to the entrance.

Disarmed by the glare, the monster was at once surrounded by his maddened adversaries, finally succumbing to the repeated thrusts of *kris* and *tumbak* (the long battle-lance), and so the village was saved. Perhaps *Pantjoran Rawana*, the source of Rawana, is also the source of the local legend.

Chinese grave

is dumped and rotting, in the wayside drain higher up. Still, it is a pretty lane, bordered by many wild flowers and the air of putrefaction disperses as we reach an open grassy area on the river banks. No one will build here: a level that is often engulfed.

A sandy stretch through elephant grass brings us to the Wos which is much wider here, the current swirling round a low bed of shingle. What a wonderful place for a picnic and swim!

On the other side the path climbs the wooded slope and there is an ancient waterspout reserved for the use of women. To the right of it is a picturesque pool and a row of spouts where the men may wash. The pool is part of a grand design, rectangular and indented into the rock face behind a meticulously sculpted colonnade. Part of the surface is decorated with radiating rafts of pink and white water-lilies. Brilliant azure and vermilion dragonflies skim swiftly to and fro. Here is the watering-place known as *Pantjoran Rawana*.

In the lengthening shadows of late afternoon, ancient moss-covered spouts and rock-hewn walls and dark folds of the encircling green curtain reflect the flickering lights of the pool. Here, too, are caves of a sort. Above the source, in the gloomy angle of the cliff face, wide black apertures frown down upon us. Symmetrically precise and evidently man-made, these intriguing structures are the cells of a former hermitage.

Or were they, in common with other regional monuments, gouged from the living rock by the finger-nails of that other fearsome man-eating giant, **Kbo Iwa**? Similar cells of unknown antiquity are widespread in the area, including those situated behind Sari (Bridge) Homestay, a stone's throw from the Campuhan bridge. Seat of an ascetic's meditation, or ogre's charnel-house, the setting remains intensely atmospheric, and we are free to wander and wonder.

From the spring we may follow the track up the steep, rocky defile mentioned earlier, to the main road. Better to go around the hermit's pool on the right up another path which winds along the slope, and climb vertically to the ornate Chinese mausoleum at the edge of the cemetery. Cremation as well as burial ground, the sparse turf is littered with the burnt remains of funerary biers and tinselled towers.

Beneath a towering, feathery-leafed **tamarind tree** are scattered brown pods containing seeds coated in a sticky bitter-sweet pulp. These may be eaten raw or served in the form of *rujak*, a salad of diced unripe fruit, spiced and sweetened with palm sugar. Chewing *pulpa tamarindorum* (which is a mild laxative), we walk past the *pura dalem* (temple of the dead). From here, we follow the paved path left (or right to Ubud) overlooking the main road and descend the long flight of steps bringing us out 100m (109yds) south of Campuhan bridge.

The Ridge

One of the most perfect bird walks, the verdant ridge is an ocean of alang-alang occasioning some delightful botanising and bird-watching. At the crest, one may view majestic Gunung Agung and a glimpse of the sea behind. Early morning or later afternoon start (to see the birds), it is an hour or so if walking only as far as the first hamlet, Bankiang Sidem. If walking on to Keliki, allow at least three hours passing through rice-fields, Bankiang Sidem and Sebali. Beyond is Taro, known for its white brahmin cattle, buff sandstone quarries and its architecture. The way is also ideal for mountain-bikes: an uninterrupted journey to Batur.

To gain the ridge, go via Pura Campuhan taking the steps leading down from the main road opposite Murni's. Pass behind the school and join the main temple approach to cross the bridge spanning the easterly stream. Instead of entering the temple complex, proceed right on the path under the temple wall. Continue through the tall

'The verdant ridge'

Yellow Rattlebox plant

grass to connect with the track which winds upward to the crown of the ridge. This is the self-same track which took us earlier to Pantjoran Widedari but we have engineered a skillful short-cut and the source of the Heavenly Nymphs is now behind us.

We may actually march without deviating from our path all the way from here to the village of Batur overlooking the great lake of the same name – a distance of some 32km (20 miles) and a full day's journey going on a newly- and partly-surfaced road further north of **Keliki.** But today we are content to amble and absorb the sights and scents wafting in the air.

Advancing to the crest, what remains of our breath is instantly snatched away by the magnificent vistas unfolding the length of the deep river valleys to either side. Here at our feet is the essential Bali. Between the temple and the first small hamlet on the ridge, there is no water course or cultivation: all is an ocean of *alang-alang*, gently billowing in the breeze as far as the eye can see.

Interspersed in the tall grass are orchids, a kind of *Spathoglottis* with buttercup yellow flowers; and a very common, small variety of **Susanna** (*Habenaria*) **orchid**, with white, deeply fringed petals, smelling strongly of vanilla. Along the wayside are clumps of **Snakeweed**, with narrow blue flowering spikes like rats' tails, and masses of yellow **Rattlebox** – in Balinese *tjereng-tjereng* – so named for its rattling seed-cases that eventually turn black.

Far below, the silver slivers of stream flash and tumble on their stony beds. Swiftlets and **swallows** skim silently through the azure arc above, while tussocks of seeding grass beside us resound with the rustle and chatter of flocks of **munias** and **weaver-birds.**

Here, too, is the haunt of the large, booming, black and chestnut ground-cuckoos, known as **coucals**, or crow-pheasants. In one sweeping gaze over the grassy slopes, we may spot several of them sitting openly on scraggy bushes in the late afternoon sun, venting their peculiar hooting calls.

A fleeting line of shadow on the path and a soft whoosh overhead announce the passage of a formation of snow-white **egrets** heading

for the communal roost at the neighbouring village of **Petulu**. The Campuhan ridge serves as the finest vantage to view several hundred stately individuals forming a mighty phalanx which reaches clear across the sky. A long, white, undulating ribbon it descends lightly on the line of

Mount Agung

Pura desa at Taro

palms adorning the eastern ridge, seemingly to become entwined, then fluttering on and fading out of sight.

The path climbs sharply to a wall of vegetation sheltering a tiny hamlet within the jurisdiction of **Bankiang Sidem**. Pausing to look east to north-east up the valley, we obtain a stunning view of the majestic mountain **Gunung Agung**, abode of the gods, soaring to the ether, wreathed in vaporous wisps. Glancing behind, with perfect visibility, we may glimpse the sea; low fringe of surf flickering on the reef; unrelieved contour of the pale lavender headland to the rear forming the southern horizon.

We have seen enough for one day; so turn about, facing the sea and saunter back the way we came.

Time permitting, we should have gone on to Keliki, via Bankiang Sidem and **Sebali**. Walking there and back on the ridge is a distance of 8km (5 miles). If our sole purpose is strict exercise, we should devote two hours at least: if bird-watching or botanising, it may take us all day.

Emerging from the first small settlement through high hedges of **pandanus** into the rice-fields, we are presented with a miracle of engineering. The twin streams flow still far below yet ways have been found to channel water to this attenuated outpost.

The main village is soon reached. Note that *sidem* is the name of a species of black ant which inhabits trees, while *bankiang* means waist or (in this case) thorax. Taking the first hamlet as the head, the fields and village proper as the abdomen, the whole assemblage, Bankiang Sidem, may simply be named after its peculiar topography.

Through the following expanse of

Star of Bethlehem

sawa, the water flows more energetically; the track is grassy and the verges abound with wild flowers, notably the shining white **Star of Bethlehem** and the elegant **Cupid's Shaving Brush** with purplish-pink florets that resemble miniature thistles.

In these surrounding villages which are relatively remote and barely accessible by motorcar, the compounds are raised on either hand. Steep-stepped entrance-ways in stone, gates and walls of adobe enclose familial *balé*, largely constructed of the same material.

Outside the village school of Sebali, situated at the southern edge of the next cultivated tract, stands a magnificent old *ficus* (**fig tree**). We stop to admire the vastly spreading exposed root system and ancient, gnarled limbs, festooned with ruddy figs, and with an epiphytic host of ferns and moss and orchids at all seasons. Our paved path leads ever gently upward, a merry torrent churning deeply in its wayside course. The cosmic mountain looms more hugely in the east.

Soon we reach the outskirts of Keliki; until recently, it was off the tarmac road. Not long ago this village was quite isolated, outsiders seldom visited or passed through but now the way is paved to **Taro** and beyond. We may choose to walk or take a bemo to that important parish, celebrated for its relict herd of white brahmin cattle, its beautiful buff sandstone quarries, and its architecture.

Legend tells us that Taro is also the former resort of Kbo Iwa, the fearful man-eating giant, for whom the inhabitants constructed a resting place. This great pavilion, which is now the *balé agung* (elders' meeting-hall) and the largest of its kind in Bali, may be inspected in the *pura desa* (a village temple that is used for all public celebrations).

At the time of a grand festival such as *Galungan*, the parade of decorations before each village gate is unusually impressive, consisting of immensely tall *penyor* (pennons of lacey palm-leaf streamers, suspended from lavishly embellished stems of bamboo) and *lamak* (long hangings of young, yellow palm-frond, fastened together with bamboo pins and elaborately patterned with stylised motifs in mature leaf of a richly contrasting dark green shade). As the *penyor* tips ought to be visible to the gods on Bali's highest mountain, so should the trailing end of each *lamak* extend from the elevated household shrine all the way to the ground.

From Taro we may return to Ubud by a scenic drive via **Pujung** and **Tegallalang**. From Keliki there is a road to Tegallalang; or we may walk west via Keliki Kawan and its monstrous banyan, and **Klusa**, making one river crossing before reaching **Payangan**. The latter is well worth a visit, with its bustling fruit and vegetable market and lovely lychee trees, situated a few kilometres by road due north of Campuhan. But I am for avoiding roads, so we return on the ridge.

The Secret Garden

👣 • Bathers

Make an early morning or mid-afternoon start and allow two or three hours if visiting Museum Neka. From Campuhan bridge descend the steps opposite Murni's towards Pura Campuhan. Skirt the temple wall and climb through the tall grass to the ridge to follow the narrow track north. The way leads to an enchanted enclave where the secret garden grows by a spring. Having admired the garden and wondered at the activities of the rock-cutters and carriers, climb to the road and seize the opportunity to view a permanent exhibition of Balinese art at Museum Neka. Return through fields across the road (opposite pura dalem Sanggingan), via Ananda Cottages to steps leading down to the main road.

All of Bali is a garden, a type of enchanted Eden made less than perfect by the hordes of emaciated, mangy dogs that wail at night as if to ward off evil spirits. Whether it is a bright vista briefly glimpsed through a moving window, or an eye-stretching panorama fixed for all time to a cinéaste's film or painter's canvas, there is everywhere a wondrous symmetry that is not the random result of unfettered natural growth.

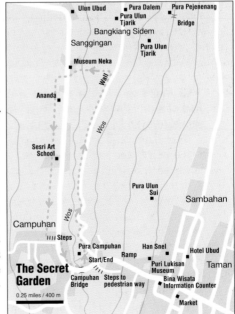

The Secret Garden

0.25 miles / 400 m

'The secret garden'

All around us is visible evidence of the regulative action of the hand of man, as well as that of God. The garden has been planted and nurtured to fruition, though by whom is seldom clear. I know of many a cultivated terrace, well-kept lawn and border and ornamental hedge, where no man ever goes. Or may be seen to go.

At a point on the ridge where the track mounts to meet the line of trees harbouring the first hamlet of Bankiang Sidem, there sits a low, overgrown retaining wall on the left. At the end of this wall, a steep path, partly concealed by the long, coarse grass, slants down the side of the gorge. Proceed cautiously along this grass-cutter's track, equally slithery when wet or dry. After one or two involuntary sittings, and sliding down the surfaces of slabs of rock, we pass through a thicket of bamboo to emerge on the sandy, shale-littered bank of the stream.

The air is cooler here. At our feet the water splashes gaily in the

shallows and over banks of shale washed down from the quarries of *paras* (soft gray sandstone of compressed volcanic ash) which line the ravine walls. The stone of this locality is said to be of superior quality, and, fashioned by adze into blocks of varying sizes, is widely employed by masons and sculptors alike.

Some of the larger blocks are crudely carved on site, destined to become guardians of temple gates, with intricate finish by craftsmen at a later date. It is not easy to transport these massive chunks of rock up perpendicular paths let into the cliff-face.

In the course of our downward slide, we could have sent a crow-pheasant sailing on rigidly outstretched wings in the form of a cross, to alight awkwardly in the undergrowth on the opposite slope. At least one kind of kingfisher flashes momentarily, shrieking, downstream: it may be the **Java Kingfisher** or the wildly loud white-collared kind (*Halcyon chloris*) – all white and turquoise with a black bill.

Butterflies too are in abundance. Prominent are the more showy birdwings and swallow-tails – *Troides helena* – very large, all black and gold with a crimson crown, soaring and dipping in erratic, fluttery flight; *Papilio memnon* – big, black and brisk, his mate paler, with pink and white markings, proceeding at a more leisurely pace; *P. peranthus* – long-tailed and dashing, with brilliant blue and green reflections.

Troides helena

I include the scientific names to aid identification in case the brief descriptions do not fit. Unlike birds, most tropical species of butterfly are not recognised by popular English or vernacular names (and even if they do have such names, they are seldom standardised, much less discussed).

On either side, the cliff-face lowers beneath a fringe of matted sprays and roots and vines; in places, faceted and boldly concave where the quarrymen have hacked away and still continue to do so, in fact. At times, weakened by undermining, the whole wall sheers off and crumbles in a massive landslip, bearing away and burying the gangs of men who labour here. Theirs is a perilous occupation.

Time to head a short way upstream. Finding a suitable place to cross where the flow is swift and shallow, we pass beneath a sharply angled escarpment on our left and then take a small path that weaves behind great tumbled boulders

Lantana

and winds along the grassy bank. The grim precipice yields to a softly rolling, lush green slope nestling in the shelter of the cliff. Here, in this enchanted enclave, our secret garden grows.

Plantain, palms and coffee bushes with shiny ribbed leaves spring up amongst mounds of moss-clad stones, bordered by bamboo and ferns and ornamental grasses. Here are scarlet hibiscus and **Flame of the Woods** (*Ixora*), pink *Melastoma*, blue **Eyebright** (*Torenia*), and yellow **Ox-Eye** (*Wedelia*); with scattered bushes of **Lantana** and **Copperleaf**. In the background, a flaming pink and green **Tree-of-Kings** (*Cordyline*) looms before a weathered shrine.

Higher up the slope, a row of slender **Coral-bean trees** (*Erythrina*) forms a striking backdrop to our garden amphitheatre showering the land below with a carpet of blood-red blossoms shaped like long sheathed talons. Often found bordering water-courses, these prickly, deciduous shedders have a bed of thorns at their base. A related, but less spiny species, is widely planted as a shade-tree in upland coffee plantations.

> Beware the wicked Tiger's Claw,
> Which, if it can, will sure stick your
> Poor feet, in case you happen by,
> And cause you forcibly to cry,
> Oh! *Erythrina indica*,
> What a ferocious brute you are!

To savour fully our surrounds, we throw ourselves down on the springy ground or loll in an eddy beneath a sun-baked rock. We may be accompanied by the limber bodies of laughing girls, reviving themselves from the exertions of carrying blocks of *paras* all day uphill. But the water here is often turbid, washing down the effluvium of excavated waste, and the bottom is littered with slimy debris. It is in the other tributary that we should take a dip, preferably another day.

We wander up the slope to the most radiant jewel of all in this fertile treasure-chest – a grove of fragrant **frangipani**, dripping with the white blooms that are used to adorn ceremonial head-dresses and the potent beard of the revered *barong*.

Behind the screen formed by this perfumed arabesque of foliage and tangled limbs, there lies a superb *pantjoran* of several spouts where we may thoroughly cleanse ourselves and drink deeply of the crystal spring. Beyond us, a short way upstream, glinting in the sunlight, the holly-green crown of a *beringin* casts its shadow over the water. There are more grottoes in the cliff behind, both naturally eroded and man-made, which we can explore now, or another day.

Above the spring, the path climbs up rocky steps where hands and knees come into play. Meanwhile the supple *paras* bearers march jauntily to the summit, heads

Yellow Ox-eye flower

laden with precariously balanced blocks, but even they may sweat and grunt, and wield a staff with which to steady themselves.

On a narrow turfed ledge the path divides – one way down to the banyan, the other up. Rest a moment for a (may it not be the) last, lingering look at the prodigal garden, flourishing unheeded, tended by unseen green fingers.

Continue upwards, on a rock-hewn staircase which gives way to steps cut into the earth. Then, mount a vertical corridor through the tall, swaying grass to until, at last, we reach the steel pipeline conveying spring water to Ubud.

Another pause for breath and contemplation before we take the track skirting the temple to the main road. Here, we have the options of catching a bemo or trudging home by road, or crossing the latter and proceeding on the wide, pastoral causeway opening directly before us.

Since we are so near, let us visit the picture gallery of **Suteja Neka** situated a few yards to the north. The complex contains a permanent exhibition of Balinese art, probably unsurpassed in scope elsewhere. It includes also a representative display of the work of expatriate artists, most notably **Bonnet**, **Hofker**, **Meier**, **Smit**, **Friend**, **Blanco** and **Snel** – but no Spies!

Recently, I spent an entire afternoon (of course, after a séance in the Secret Garden) in a room filled with the ravishing watercolours and pastels of the Dutch painter Willem Hofker, who captures with equal and enviable facility the not insubstantial forms of either Bali belles or crumbling temple gates.

To return to Campuhan, enter the broad ride opposite *pura dalem* **Sanggingan**, which leads

Indian almond and clove trees

to a well-wooded cemetery. Note the **Indian Almond** (*Terminalia catappa*) tree, the largest of its kind that I have seen. Smaller versions of these trees are often seen on the coast. The Indian Almond tree, in its earlier stages, is remarkable for the growth of its spreading branches in layered concentric rings but the distinctive pattern disappears with maturity. The leaves which are shed twice annually, turn a handsome rich red before they fall together with the almond-shaped fruits. If we take a nut and crack it open, we will be pleasantly surprised to discover that it tastes like an almond too.

Having gorged ourselves on almonds, we follow the narrow (and normally muddy) path through the wood, bounding on conveniently placed boulders across the small stream, and climb up to the *sawa*. Turn sharply left, and, keeping the stream always on our left, head south on the raised bund which carries the main irrigation channel.

Vanilla pods

This brings us to a mixed spice plantation of **clove** and **vanilla.** The cloves are borne on conical bushy trees whose leaves range in colour from pink to dark glossy green. The vanilla in the form of fleshy green orchids climbs on poles; the famous flavouring being obtained by a long and intricate processing of the fruiting capsules. We may not have seen the growing plants before so it is as well that we recognise them now. As we squeeze between the clustered stems, we suddenly emerge at the head of a flight of crazy-paved steps descending to a swimming-pool.

This pool, beautifully situated in the fields and abutting on a restful lawn, belongs to **Ananda Cottages.** If we cannot restrain the impulse to jump in, we should settle the entrance fee at the reception desk near the road on the other side of the stream. Down the steps, past the pump-house, and under a row of vicious coral-beans, the path leads up and over an embankment supporting an overhead water conduit. Continue through a narrow strip of pasturage following the course of the stream.

Soon we come to a concrete weir and chute draining into an abysmally deep gully. Ignoring the latter, we advance in a straight line to the next expanse of *sawa*, and pass beneath an immensely high hedge of hibiscus. The fields hereabout are rapidly being replaced by new buildings, and before we know it, our grassy trail is cemented over, and we are actually in the forecourt of a restaurant, where we may or may not choose to have a meal and a drink.

On to the main track which leads to the northern *banjar* of Penestanan, we go left, down the broad flight of many steps which brings us back to the main road just north of Hotel Campuhan.

Stone sculpture, Ananda Cottages

The Meeting Pool

👣 • Bathers • Picnic • Sarong

Begin preferably early morning, allowing three hours if bathing. From Campuhan bridge via Pura Campuhan on to the ridge, cross the eastern valley at the first small settlement of Bankiang Sidem. Descending the hillside to the river's edge, the path leads to an isolated pool, the meeting pool, forged by foaming rapids. It is a place unfrequented by Man except for farmers and fishermen and the animals who come to frolic and refresh themselves. After the bathe, wade across the river and inspect Pura Ulun Tjarik before returning through fields to a ramp by an aqueduct, and down to the main road.

Half an hour's brisk stroll will bring us to the pool which lies in the valley formed by the eastern tributary of the Wos. Instead of leaving the ridge on the grass-cutter's path, which took us into the western valley and the Secret Garden, we continue into the hamlet, pausing to turn and direct our gaze to the distant sea before entering the shade.

Only a few metres short of the next open patch of *sawa*, a lane leads right, through a gap in the *pandanus*

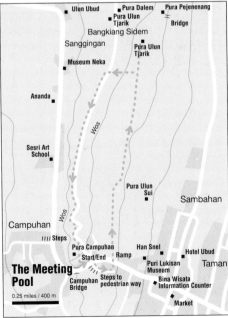

41

Melastoma flower

(screw pine) hedge to a domestic compound. This we follow, skirting the buildings on our left, down four steps then making a fairly steep descent of the hillside.

At the foot of the incline we pass an unwalled enclosure, consisting of a small house and some outhouses. Reclining on a crude palm-thatched (*atap*) *balé*, seemingly in an eternal state of siesta, are several contented piebald goats. Handsome, sturdy beasts they are, and one cannot help comparing their enviable condition with that of the gaunt refuse-sifting creatures which inhabit waste-ground, rubbish tips and railway depots elsewhere. The sleek devils regard us silently with a malignant cast in their diabolic eyes.

Tripping lightly down terraces of dry cultivation, following in the wake of watering cattle, through layers of scrubby growth and flowering bushes of *Lantana*, dazzling **White Flag** (*Mussaenda*), and pretty pink *Melastoma*, with its pulpy purplish black fruits – seedy but perfectly edible – we come shortly to the water's edge.

From here, we can see our path continuing on the other side. Later, we shall wade almost up to our waists to cross this stream. Meanwhile, it is time for a swim, and the Meeting Pool awaits temptingly 20m (22yds) upstream.

Enroute to the Meeting Pool

Skipping easily along the bank behind one or two sun-warmed boulders, we arrive at a gentle bend in the river beneath a sheer, towering cliff. At our feet lies a thick border of bright yellow Ox-eye, freer and more exuberant than in a formal garden.

And here is our pool, wide and sandy-bottomed, transparent and sparkling, forged by the foaming rapids at its head. There is no one about but the tingling sensation of sudden and rapid flight, on swift pattering feet or silently flexing wings, substantial or imaginary, lingers in the still air.

Here, have I surprised the **otter** and the **civet** (*lubak*), and the giant **monitor lizard** (*aloo*); and the wilder birds, including **Junglefowl** (*Gallus varius*) and **Forktail** (*Enicurus leschenaultii*). For the dogs, it is definitely their preferred watering-hole.

Had we approached more discreetly, might we not have glimpsed **Supraba** the nymph, surrounded by her celestial train, attending to her daily ablutions?

Having taken off our clothing and placed it on a convenient slab of rock to air in the sun, and shielding ourselves with unaffected

modesty, we step into the deep pool and joyfully surrender ourselves to the water's healing embrace.

Anchor yourself on a submerged ledge, astride the full flow of the cascade where the stream tumbles as in a millrace, through crevices in the projecting teeth of the ever-shifting natural barrage.

The body takes a pummelling equal to, but more evenly distributed than that administered by the trained hands of a masseur. It can be varied in direction and intensity, instantly and at will. It is the most invigorating type of physiotherapy that I know of sitting in mid-stream, spread-eagled in the surf and sun – and it will not cost you a penny!

A giant refreshed from the torrential force or from merely basking in the sun-drenched pool, we gather our bundle of well-aired clothing and return to where the track meets the river. Wade across, taking care not to skid on the smooth banks of layered tuff nor be punctured by the sharp spines of tiger's claws lying in wait along

the way.

Dressed once more, we climb the turf-clad hillside, giving a wide berth to the tethered cows and calves, which are not accustomed to the sight and smell of foreigners. At the top, the way leads through the yard of a cosy mud-brick *pondok* or cabin designed to house farming implements, fertiliser, and fodder, and to provide a temporary shelter whilst working in the fields.

Between clove plantation and rice terrace, the path now levels on a well-worn bund bordered on one side by a bank of waving *alang-alang*, until the principal artery is reached. Before heading for home, take a quick look at the little temple, sacred to the rice goddess **Dewi Sri**.

Known as Pura Ulun Tjarik (in high Balinese, literally temple at the head of the rice-fields), and one of the prettiest sanctuaries I have seen, the small walled enclosure sits on the lip of the valley, 100m (109yds) toward the north. Two beautifully-wrought shrines for offerings (*apit lawang*) of brick and stone, stand on either side of the pylon or split gate (*candi bentar*): inside are more pavilions (*balé*) and shrines, one thatched, all with evidence of offerings freshly made.

All are sumptuously sculpted amidst a garden of scarlet hibiscus and **Cardinal's Hat**, **Blue Trumpet Vine** (*Thunbergia*) and golden **Allamanda**, and, most amazing of all, a mass of rich, pink **cabbage-roses.** Standing nearby are three gnarled frangipanis and a sweetly-scented flowering **Champak tree** (*Michelia*). A few paces further on, pause by clumps of pink *Melastoma* for a last, long look down the verdant slopes of this spectacular gorge.

There is Bali for you!

The way home is south to Ubud. Without deviating from the main path through the fields, we come finally to a wide ramp leading down to the main road.

Supraba

Supraba the Nymph and Rajapala

You must have noticed the lovely scene, so often depicted in Balinese paintings. Mortal **Rajapala**, having wandered undetected into the presence of the bathing nymph Supraba and been smitten by her charms, is suddenly perceived by her in the very act of stealing her *selendang* (scarf), which represents her wings. It is too late! He has possession of her only means of escape from earth. Her earnest entreaties are of no avail; and in the end she is persuaded to remain with Rajapala, on the condition of her bearing him a son, before she may finally return to heaven.

Ulun Ubud

👣 • Bathers

Commence after lunch, allowing three or four hours if pausing for refreshments at Ulun Ubud. From Campuhan bridge via Pura Campuhan on Campuhan ridge, through first settlement to main village of Bankiang Sidem. Opposite Pura Dalem, cross the edge of fields behind Pura Ulun Tjarik to view the spectacular wedding-cake tiers of the palace on the scarp. Then down the stream and up the gorge to the delightful surprises of Ulun Ubud hotel. Home by road or through fields roughly parallel via Ananda Cottages and steps to main road.

Approaching Bankiang Sidem proper, after crossing the first stretch of rice-fields, the path winds in an S-bend from which a track leads right to the Pura Dalem. To the left there is no clearly defined public way, only an irrigation channel and a muddy bank. Nonetheless, we head left, climbing up to the level of the *sawa* and proceeding along its edge behind the temple Pura Ulun Tjarik.

Selecting the driest and widest balks nearest to the hedge, notice

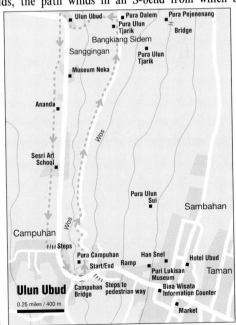

Stone flowers, Ulun Ubud Hotel

a gap in the latter a few terraces from the rim of the valley. On climbing through, we find ourselves in somebody's back garden and, moreover, on a dry (if it has not been raining), well-trodden path leading down to a bamboo thicket. Take care not to frighten the cows tethered nearby and pass under the bamboo to come out in the open at the edge of the great divide.

If anything, the rift here is more spectacular than ever, and the luxuriant growth crowns frowning rock walls, inexorably hacked to pieces by the quarrymen on either side.

What is truly startling is the scarp before us; the extraordinary, dream-like edifice ascending in wedding-cake tiers, pink and white and gleaming. How came this gilded palace transposed from the pages of a fairytale treasury, if not by some supernatural agency – by the hand of Kbo Iwa? It would seem to call for closer investigation but first we must overcome the great divide.

The path descends abruptly, but not perilously, down a grassy slope dotted with shrubs and stunted trees. Here too is the haunt of **Green Junglefowl** (*Gallus varius*) and monstrous monitor lizard which I have often put to flight in my precipitate career. Negotiating

a final defile in the cliff face, and clambering down a rocky shoulder, we attain the fragmented riverbed.

Cautiously picking our way across the shallow stream, we ascend over a mass of scree and up rough stone steps, pausing every now and then to survey the fantastic vistas up and down the gorge. And we wonder at the tenacious dedication of the men who labour under the ever-present shadow of impending avalanche.

Past sculpted columns behind which grottoes yawn, we scramble doggedly upward under the angle of a high stone wall to the foot of a tremendously high man-made staircase. Mounting the first few steps, we spy an entrance in the wall immediately to our left. The wicket-gate is open: no *cave canem* ("Beware of dog") sign glowers from the lintel, so we go in.

The transformation is as total as it is unexpected, and it is not mere bodily exertion that causes us to tremble at the knees. We feel as Alice must have felt when she emerged from that dark corridor into the enchanted garden.

A shimmering swimming-pool reposes beside a trim lawn, under the soaring citadel which seems to emanate from the Arabian Nights. We stand entranced, feet stuck in the icing that adorns the bottom layer of the giant's nuptial cake. This is the place known as **Ulun Ubud** (*ulun*, the head) – a small, delightful hotel situated in Sanggingan, which may be considered as the head, as Campuhan is the neck, of the mayoralty of Ubud.

Provided we are not too dishevelled or insolvent, I propose a cooling drink to be sipped leisurely at the poolside bar, followed by a swim, and perhaps another drink, before we order a taxi to take us home.

If we are in need of further exercise, we should scurry up the steps and down the driveway to the main road. Instead of traipsing along the latter, we can cut through the fields bordering the village on a broad bund beside the main watercourse which runs more or less parallel to the road. Crossing a deep ditch which dissects the *sawa*, and turning left, we very soon find ourselves on the other side of the graveyard spinney, where stands the Indian Almond tree we saw on our return from the Secret Garden. And the rest of the way is easy.

Valley, Ulun Ubud

Subak

Allow up to four hours, beginning early morning or afternoon – longer if taking refreshment at Han Snel's. From Campuhan bridge go towards Ubud (climbing steps to pedestrian way above main road), then cross road under aqueduct and up ramp into fields. Follow the path past Pura Ulun Tjarik to Pura Pejenenang, crossing ravine on concrete bridge and follow the path south through fields to the instructive Subak temple – Pura Ulun Sui. Behold the ragged scarecrows, the shrines, the interweaving irrigation channels, the offerings and farming implements that are essentially Balinese. Proceed to Puri Lukisan Museum of Art or deviate via Han Snel's to the main road.

Having devoted the best part of several days to exploring the Campuhan ridge, it is time to adopt a new tack. Today, we wander past Murni's towards Ubud, mounting the flight of steps on the right, where the road begins to incline up the long cutting. Trucks

Subak sawa

and buses, bikes and bemos hurtle all day long on this route belching infernal fumes; besides which, to walk on the road is frankly hazardous.

The cement footpath continues above the traffic at the same level as the *sawa* on the other side, and that is where we wish to be. To arrive there, take a clever shortcut by crawling along the overhead water conduit that spans the road – do not be alarmed for I have often run this way! Or be more prudent and descend the steps, passing under the aqueduct, and ascending the wide, cobbled ramp to the fields.

Following the path left, proceed past a rather odd-looking, two-storeyed building set in an ornamental garden, and overshadowed by a grotesque water-tower. Clearly, it is not a Balinese abode.

Entering the fields which stretch before us in an uninterrupted swath to the northern horizon, we cast our eyes about us, but the view to the west presents a very different picture. In the background, the ridge which reveals its fertile slope to the inhabitants of Penestanan has all but vanished under the oppressive weight of suburban development.

Intervening in the foreground, lies the *alang-alang* wreathed brow of our familiar Campuhan ridge. Surely, none may impose his new design for living here. No water, for a start.

Turning to our immediate vicinity, we note the varying stages of growth of different strains of rice. Beyond, and quite outstanding, is the tall and elegant *jogading* (traditional Balinese rice) with long, white, whiskery ears. Much-prized and increasingly scarce, it requires a relatively long growth yielding at most two crops per year.

Contrast it to the other strain, drab and stunted, which seems to compose most of the acreage hereabout. This, I am told, rejoices in the style of PB5, which even now is being phased out and replaced by R36, or it

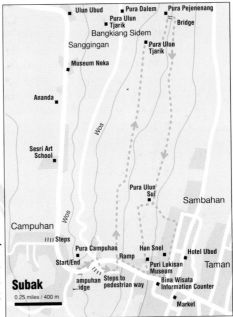

Subak

0.25 miles / 400 m

49

Attap hut in padi field

may be R64 – high yield and producing three crops at least.

Critics often question the introduction of these laboratory-processed rice strains in terms of labour and energy expended. They worry about the use of pesticides and artificial fertilisers, the consequent depletion of the soil, and the quality of nutriment.

Moreover, there is consideration of the upset of the natural cycle that revolves around the ordained seasons; the devastation of the lives of insects and birds. It is not uncommon to see many unfledged, tiny **fantail warblers** (*Cisticola* species which nest in, but do not harm, the rice-crop), staggering through the stubble, dispossessed by the reaper's sickle long before their prime.

Afflicted by thoughts such as these, we wend our way through the padi. Here and there are flimsy little huts, chiefly made of *attap* (palm thatch) and *bedeg* (plaited bamboo), and usually supported at either end by a living tree. Called *kubu*, being somewhat smaller than a *pondok*, these cabins may be used for rest and refreshments in the heat of the day. They are usually used to provide cover for the young manipulators of the cords that set in motion various devices for shooing the birds. And by the same token they make marvellous hides.

The scarecrows themselves draw our attention being as variform as they are unequal in efficacy. Often have I started in mid-stride, seized by an awful foreboding of some preterhuman presence, only to find myself confronted by an unseeing concoction of cast-off rags, artfully suspended from a bamboo scaffold.

Apart from lifelike scarecrows,

Working in ricefield

there is a network of lines and bunting criss-crossing the *sawa*, which nowadays often consists of magnetic tape or wire with tin-cans and sheets of plastic attached – such is progress! Then there are marvellous contraptions utilising wind-driven blades, equipped with cams and trip-hammers, which create a merry racket. In the end there is really no effective substitute for the hollering of farmers' lads, or the brisk clacking of hand-held rattles and slapsticks.

Farther on, the fields lie fallow and flooded; a vast, glittering mosaic that mirrors the fleeting white clouds and sentinel palms whilst muting all else is the sound of rushing water – water, the source of all life.

Water in abundance is fundamental to the growth of rice, as rice itself is fundamental to the existence of the Balinese. Arguably, the paramount institution in Bali is the Subak, which may be defined as a society or co-operative of landowners whose prime concern is the efficient and equitable distribution of water. And viewing the unevenness of the terrain around us, we may well ask how on earth all this water came to be here in the first place. The answer is: by the most elaborate system of elevated, surface, and subterranean aqueducts ever devised by man – a miracle of engineering for you!

'The Balinese are famed as the most efficient rice-growers in the archipelago. They raise two crops of fine rice a year with such success that they have more than sufficient for the needs of the population, often having enough left over to sell or give away. Even agricultural experts admit that modern methods could not improve the already excellent results, due perhaps to the intense striving of the Balinese for improvement, their communal, co-operative agricultural societies, and their Burbank-like system of seed selection,' said Miguel Covarrubias in 1934.

The path continues north through steep banks festooned with ferns and overhung by young coconut palms on either side. A sense of *déjà vu* prevails; there are other similar passages but coming

Even as I write, things change…

There was an old woman – now alas! confined to her compound – who kept her *pondok* and modest strip of land atop the Penestanan ridge. She would always give the children little presents of *jagung* (sweet-corn) or *tebuh* (sugar-cane), and sometimes we would take her a parcel of *kopi* (coffee) and *gula* (granulated sugar).

My most vivid memory is of the incredible collection of scarecrows she was forever assembling – a whole battalion of them, tricked out in every conceivable kind of garb, and staked out in rows to protect the property on all sides. She was delightfully dotty – one might truly say 'mad as a hatter!' – and I know that her creations made far more of an impression on us than on the munias and weavers they were meant to keep at bay. Sadly, that tattered guard no longer adorns the skyline, and the plot has been swallowed by a complex of holiday bungalows.

'Scarecrow'

Pura Pejenengan

into the open, we realise at once that we have been this way before, in the opposite direction, on our return from the Meeting Pool. Here is the temple of Dewi Sri with its garden of roses and shining trumpets though the way ahead is new.

Walk on northwards, keeping the racing watercourse on our right side. Note the trees with very large leaves. These are **Breadfruit** (*Artocarpus* species), known locally as *timbul*. Several fine specimens raise their crowns above the wall of vegetation sprouting from the gully on the right. The path now swings obliquely across the *sawa* to continue on that side.

We stop to admire the glorious pedestal **Pura Pejenengan** erected wholly in stone, framed by twining frangipani, and fronted by a hibiscus hedge. Look about; not a discordant note. Vaguely looming to the south, the sea and Benoa Bay and red-roofed resorts dotting the *bukit*.

About 200 years ago, Captain Bligh set sail from Tahiti with a cargo of breadfruit trees on board his ship *Bounty*, bound for the West Indies. Shortly after, the famous mutiny occurred, but the captain survived to lead another expedition, successfully bringing breadfruit to the New World.

The muffled roar of water cascading into a deep chasm now reaches our ears, and through the spreading plantain, a bridge with blue-painted railings is briefly glimpsed. A few metres more, and we take the track that winds down to cross the ravine. We walk over on the natural grassy arch nearby, pausing to marvel at the depth of this narrow gulf and at the profusion and variety

Chasing dragonflies

of plant-life issuing forth.

Butterflies are abundant here. Observe the black-veined, blue and tawny crows and tigers (*Danaidae* family), and the **Malayan Lacewing** (*Cethosia bibliosi*), which is a brilliant fox-red suffused with lilac above, and an amazing zigzag pattern resembling batik below. This is one of the few places I know where you can be fairly certain of seeing this elusive species whose caterpillars feed on the wild **passion-fruit** vines which flourish rampantly here.

Look out for the *Troides* as well – huge and black and golden: its foodplant is another family of vines, the poisonous, strangling *Aristolochia*, normally grubbed out by farmers but allowed to proliferate here.

Proceed south along the earthy track with a newly-constructed irrigation channel on the left, chasm at the right, and see how the former disappears and reappears through a series of underground tunnels. Consider, too, how gangs of men, equipped only with picks and shovels, remain in constant thrall, scrabbling like moles or hobbits, beneath the surface of the earth.

Tropical fruit

Many different kinds of fern, grass, shrub, and orchid, spring and droop from the high bank. Still more creep and spray from the dizzy depths below. Rounding a bend, we emerge into the open, and the gorge drops away to the right beside a grove of **jackfruit** trees (also *Artocarpus*), called *nangka* by the Balinese.

The enormous *nangka* fruits, often bagged against the depredations of birds and insects and grubby, prying fingers, erupt and hang directly from the bole and older branches. One fruit can weigh as much as one hundredweight (50 kg). It can be eaten either ripe, or unripe as a delicious vegetable (*jukut nangka*). The seeds may be boiled or roasted similarly to chestnuts.

The sticky latex exuding from the fruit and tree is put to several uses: children smear it on long poles for catching dragonflies, while some larger people (who ought to know better!) prepare bird-lime from it for trapping birds.

Beneath the *nangka* are cowsheds, and scattered about, their tethered complement of oxen. Clad in immaculate white socks and displaying almost immaculate white bottoms, they are direct descendants of the wild *banteng,* which may still be found in the forests of north-west Bali. In the foreground, an immense *tjangin* (coralbean or tiger's-claw), is smothered in ferns and lichens and **dog-orchids** (*angrek tjitjing*) and other epiphytic plants. Watch your feet!

Now the fields stretch ahead, yet again manifesting different stages

of *padi* growth, and above the bickering of the water, hear the tinkling and clicking of tiny, tumbling fantail-warblers, exhorting the reapers to stay the cutting and spare their fledglings in the nest.

By the offerings laid out at the edge of one ripe patch, we can tell that the harvest is imminent. Normally, there are the little palm-leaf plaited trays of spices and fruit and rice, together with the odd Chinese coin (*kepeng*), brilliantly-coloured blossoms, and palm-leaf cut-outs representing faces or formed into *tjili* (stylised female figures denoting Dewi Sri).

Now besides all these, stand two sheaves of rice fastened together, one said to be male and the other female. This is known as the rice mother – **nini pantun** – which following the harvest, is decorated and dressed up before being blessed in a special ceremony and stored in the family granary. There are other offerings at other stages of development, always remarkable for the touch of grace and gaiety and colour they add to the rice-fields in every season.

A particular and prevalent feature is the row of *tugu*, little shrines placed at regular intervals through the fields, usually corresponding with the direction of the main watercourse and pedestrian way.

Scattered as far as the eye can see are lovely affairs of warm red brick, topped with roofs of durable, black palm-fibre (*idjuk*), each with its own little garden of marigold or periwinkle or other brilliant bloom.

These are known as *sanga limas* or *sanga tjutjuk* (*tugu* being the generic term for shrine), more pleasing to look at than the tawdry prefabricated cement jobs which seem to be taking over wherever

Pura ulun sui, or temple of the agricultural guild

Puri Lukisan Museum of Art

the pressures and distractions of modern living consume the time devoted to the making of beautiful things.

Down through the fields, water tumbling at every bend, perfect vista of open slope and palm; consecrated to the rice goddess, more everlasting shrines. I have never seen a prettier path than this.

Here come the first pagodas – bright coral pink and upstanding, poised high above a bed of heart-shaped leaves. We may have seen *Clerodendrum paniculatum,* the **Pagoda Flower,** in formal gardens, but never in a setting such as this. Now we stroll through borders of breathtaking splendour – **croton**, copperleaf, cordyline, **poinsettia**, clove, hibiscus. Lofty pagodas dominating all. Show me the author of this floral pageant, gentle genius of this grand design.

A walled temple enclosure and other buildings appear to the right of our garden path. Pura Ulun Tjarik again? But the compound is set in the heart of the fields. This is the temple of the *subak* or agricultural guild, known generally as *pura bedugul* and *pura ulun sui*, as a stylishly lettered sign points out quite clearly.

All things here are sacred to Sri. If we look about us, we shall see that everything is neatly labelled – the tower where the *kulkul* (alarm drums) are housed, and the *lumbung* (granary) where the rice is stored. We are standing by the temple and secular offices of the *subak* of **Juwukmanis**, which is situated on the Gunung Agung side of the Campuhan river. All about us are models of construction.

We now have a choice: museum or refreshment? Perhaps we can manage both. The long red catkins of the **Chenille Plant** wave farewell as we proceed at right angles to the main track, past the *kulkul* and *kantor*, on a wide, grassy bund. Turning left down another avenue of young palms and herbaceous borders, we find ourselves behind the Puri Lukisan Museum of Art. Follow the wall around and enter the garden which is well worth inspecting, as are the various

Cloves

55

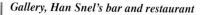

Gallery, Han Snel's bar and restaurant

exhibits in several pavilions, scattered over a broad area. Finally, when exiting by the main entrance, remember that we have not paid any admission fees and we should make amends accordingly.

If refreshments is the priority, do not deviate from the path but continue past the temple and down a slight gradient, lined by clove-trees (*tjingké*) to cross a concrete bridge. Then, bearing right, follow the path into the northern *banjar* of Ubud.

For the adventurous, I might propose one last diversion. Less than 100m (109yds) after the bridge, by a small, white-washed shed, take the track on the right. This brings us to a concrete irrigation channel issuing from a tunnel where the usual bevy of belles is doing the washing. A few more paces, and the opening on the right leads to a profound flight of steps carved from the living rock. These we descend with some trepidation, all other sound blotted out by the roar of the great chute at our rear.

Joining the river, and provided it is not in spate, we hasten along the banks, under sheer rock walls, until we reach a small waterfall and narrow cleft through which the river gushes. Scrambling on a rocky ledge above the fall, we drop down into and wade through the stream which is not as deep as it looks. Then, dashing up another steep stairway similar to the last, we emerge into the open. After walking a few metres further on, we find ourselves back on the main thoroughfare.

Panting now with thirst and exertion, we proceed in a direct line to **Han Snel's** bar and restaurant – a restful oasis of tranquillity, and one of the most civilised watering-holes that I know of.

A flight of steps carved from the rock

A Host of White Egrets

Allow three hours if walking one-way – five hours for two way – which permits viewing time in the late afternoon at the heronry, the primary objective of the itinerary. Start at 1 to 2pm from Campuhan bridge to the ramp by the aqueduct, then north through fields all the way to Kelabangmuding. Heading east and skirting Banjar Abangan, join the asphalt road north of Petulu to spend 30 minutes observing white egrets. Return to Ubud by way of Pura Dalem Jungungan and Banjar Kutuh Kaja and Banjar Kutuh Klod. If you take a longer time at the heronry, return to Ubud by road.

From Campuhan, go back towards Ubud and ascend the cobbled ramp which leads to the rice-fields from under the aqueduct. Then heading north, continue through the fields past Pura Ulun Tjarik set in its pretty garden. About a few hundred metres further on we glimpse the little bridge with blue railings spanning the ravine, hoping that the railings have not been painted green or rusted away entirely since. Do not cross over but continue north, line of lush vegetation sprouting from the abyss at our right, *sawa* at our left.

Irrespective of season, somewhere between Campuhan and **Kelabangmuding**, there should be flooded ter-

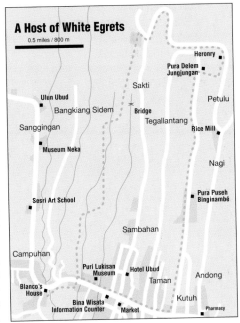

A Host of White Egrets

0.5 miles / 800 m

Heronry

Pura Delem Jungjungan

Sakti

Petulu

Ulun Ubud

Bangkiang Sidem

Bridge

Tegallantang

Sanggingan

Rice Mill

Museum Neka

Nagi

Sesri Art School

Pura Puseh Binginambé

Sambahan

Campuhan

Puri Lukisan Museum

Hotel Ubud

Taman

Andong

Blanco's House

Kutuh

Bina Wisata Information Counter

Market

Pharmacy

Breeding Cattle Egret

races with ducks disporting on them. It is especially in this stretch that I have seen enormous flocks – numbering many hundreds – being fattened for the pot. The local delicacy is smoked and spiced duck; you have to place your order 24 hours ahead to experience this gastronomic treat.

Ducks there are in abundance. Some birds regard us quizzically, as if deciphering our thoughts. Beside them, fenced against their intrusion, brilliant emerald triangle turns out to be a nursery of rice seedlings being nurtured in preparation for transplantation.

Note the extreme narrowness of this ridge, in places no more than the width of one small strip of *sawa*. Pause to inspect the fantastic vistas on our left.

Eight hundred metres (½ mile) later, the ridge broadens a bit. Our path swings right and heads up through the heart of the fields. By a cement *tugu* we cross a minor irrigation channel with perhaps 800m (872yds) more to Kelabangmuding. Veering again to the right-hand side of the *sawa*, the path follows the irrigation channel which is presently, by a feat of extraordinary engineering, concreted for a distance of 50m (55yds) or so on the elevated bund. Below, another path leads right, over a fearfully narrow aqueduct to **Bentuyung** and the asphalt road. This way is not recommended!

Wherever we go in the rice-fields, we cannot fail to observe one butterfly in particular, the bright rust *Precis almana*, with beautiful ocellations of a lustrous purple tinge, putting one in mind of the **European Peacock** (*Vanessa io*). Momentarily lost in admiration of a brilliantly fresh specimen, it dawns on us that we have walked the best part of 3km (2 miles) through one of the most populous parts

'Ducks there are in abundance'

of Bali, without seeing a single building. That is not bad going at all!

But now our little track debouches on a broader one, and entering the outskirts of Kelabangmuding a few moments later, we are again dazzled by a field of fiery scarlet and orange **heliconia**, bordering the village cemetery (*kuburan*).

In the overgrown coppice a grove of **sago palms** spreads huge, dark green fronds, dominated by a *beringin* and two tall *pulé* trees. From the palms is derived *idjuk*, the black thatching fibre. Known locally as *jakuh*, they yield also an attractive dark-grained hardwood widely used for making tool handles, palm-sugar and toddy. It is the pith of the tree that is processed into sago flour, and more commonly fermented to produce an evil-smelling substance, doled out daily as an additive to accelerate the fattening of ducks.

The *pulé* (*Alstonia scholaris*) tree – I do not know the English name if there is one – like frangipani, is of the dogbane family, exuding a sticky white latex, and the wood is used for carving masks. Enormous specimens may be seen near cemeteries and temples.

Passing a splendid *pura dalem*, overshadowed by another massive *beringin*, we enter the village, an agreeable, tranquil place, with exceptionally fine gates of brick and *paras*. Did I say tranquil? It was until the dogs spotted me, and *my* dogs! Since my last visit electric cables and poles have been installed and soon the blacktop road will come.

Leaving Kelabangmuding, we turn right at the T-junction and curious concrete *kulkul* stand, and continue into the fields: elaborate, newly-walled conduit under a long line of palms on our left: past the rice-mill and mountain of husks: then left, not entering *banjar* **Abangan**, on a wide earthy track undulating for a few hundred metres: and unexpectedly we are back on bitumen.

The way to **Gunung Petulu**, where the white birds are, is right. It is not too bad on the road, a little over 800m (875yds), and only light traffic. But, after several minutes, arriving at a bridge and bend in the road, overlooked by a small *ulun tjarik* temple, we take a more pleasant detour. Climb up to the temple: not a bird can be seen from here. Then cut across the *sawa*.

Going to the eastern edge of the fields, then proceeding south on a fairly well-defined path, about half way to Petulu there is another track leading down to the dizziest, deepest ravine of them all, spanned by an incredible bamboo bridge, supported by the roots of a giant *beringin* at either end. This, I am told, is the way to **Sapat**.

Pressing on, the path rejoins the bitumen at *pura desa* Petulu under the umbrella of the huge *ficus*, showering the road with rotting figs. Now it is asphalt all the way. And many of the wayside trees, where formerly the egrets nested, have been chopped down and replaced by telegraph poles.

While there are still many birds in evidence, the population has clearly declined, the greater part of it retreating away from the road. However, if we wander to the other end of the village, we shall have ample opportunity to observe a number of birds at close quarters, and more are arriving every minute.

Briefly, there are three types of white heron or egret roosting and nesting here; and the period of greatest activity is from January to August, though unfledged birds may be seen pretty well throughout the year. There are **Cattle Egrets** (*Bubulcus ibis*), many with ginger splotches; **Little Egrets** (*Egretta garzetta*), with long, fine black bills

Rest on these steps while I tell you a bird story

One day not so long ago, whilst sitting in this very spot engrossed in my observations, I was surrounded by a bunch of boys, all of whom evidently found the activities of the funny white man in their midst far more entertaining than those of the white birds.

Suddenly, the grubbiest one of them let out a terrific yell, and tore off towards a nearby thicket. Looking up, I saw at once the object of his excited attention: an immature egret had toppled from its nest and been caught, flapping and squawking, in the upper branches of a dreaded thorny coral-bean tree. To my astonishment, quite wittingly, the reckless imp shinnied up the tree in a thrice, grabbed the bird, and before you could say 'Hold on, have a care!' was back on the ground again.

Blood streaming from his hands and feet, smothered from head to toe with viciously biting red soldier–ants, he evinced not the slightest discomfort, but swaggered over, wild-eyed and exultant. He had his bird!

I turned to address an older man who, as it turned out, was the young fellow's father.

'Will he keep the *kokokan*?' I enquired. The white egrets are collectively known by the name *kokokan*.

'No,' came the perfunctory reply.

'Well, will he sell it then?' I knew that some wretched birds are palmed off on unsuspecting tourists for a pittance.

'Oh no,' said the father, "he will eat it!"

'Good God!' said I. 'He will have *kokokan goreng* then?'

'No, no, no!' came the reply. '*Pesen kokokan.*'

Pesen, I should explain, is a sort of paste of hashed meat and herbs, cooked *en papillote*, which in Bali means wrapped in plantain leaf. *Pâté d'aigrette*, I reflected how utterly vile! And as if to echo my thought, the bird promptly regurgitated a large frog on the doorstep.

'But surely,' I continued, 'these birds are sacred?'

'Oh no,' rejoined the parent emphatically: 'Not when they fall from the nest, they are not!'

As the blossoms of jasmine tumbled to the earth may not be used in offerings, so does the dispossessed squab forfeit its sanctity. Fair game, I dare say. And on that somewhat distasteful note, I took my leave.

60

Egret

and black legs, pure white and often with two pendant head plumes; and **Short-billed Egrets** (*Egretta intermedia*), somewhat larger than the others, also pure white, usually with yellowish, dark-tipped bills and billowing breast plumes. The stunning spectacle of a vast host of wonderfully elegant snow-white birds is well worth tramping any distance to see.

With perhaps 90 minutes of daylight remaining, it is time to set off for *banjar* **Kutuh**, Ubud, unless we prefer to return by road.

Where the fields begin again on the right, by the round water-tank, we advance down and up steps in a shady lane, and out into the *sawa* by a row of sheltering palms. We then cross a minor dam, heading left (south) along the edge of the paddy. Stop and look back at the village: see those trees in the background decorated with blobs of white fleece, like trees upon an alpine slope. One snow-capped banyan stands out above the rest. Now more and more birds come, drifting flotillas in the sky: the mantle grows whiter yet. We must press on, selecting a suitable balk and crossing the field on our right, to the next line of palms, then heading south again on the track beneath them.

A few hundred metres more, and we bear right at a junction, the path leading through the *sawa* down to a marvellous bathing-shed. From **Nagi** and **Junjungan** they come to wash and fetch water: there are compartments for boys and girls. Then up the great stone steps to the top of the opposing slope, and into a sea of *padi Bali asli* – real Bali rice!

Youngsters near Ubud

Skirting the *kuburan* and *pura dalem* Jungungan, we rest for a second in the temple's outer court to admire a fine sculpture of a man surrounded by children, probably a representation of **Pan Bruyut** who, like the old woman who lived in a shoe, had so many children he knew not what to do! Such a peaceful place.

Then south on the main thoroughfare through the fields: a good long sweep, with beautiful Bali rice all the way. The people in these few villages are dour, if not uncivil, and a law unto themselves. They persist in the old ways as if the rest of Ubud did not exist. Indifferent to the new economic order, modern communications, and family planning, they remain aloof, and plant what they please; and they do not cremate their dead.

Observe now the soft sunlight of fading afternoon, the subtle tones of green and gold – pale, wispy *jogading* (actually a contraction of *hidjo* and *gading*, green and creamy yellow): all Nature is restored.

One final stop at *pura puseh binginambé*, an unusually large and spreading champak tree (*tjampaka*) lending fragrance to its court. Through the north ward – *banjar* Kutuh *kaja* – and the intervening fields to *banjar* Kutuh *klod*, where game-cocks spar earnestly, albeit spurless, in the middle of the dusty way. So we join the main road south of Ubud market.

Sculpture,
Pura Dalem
Junjungan

To The Elephant Cave via Kalebutan Hermitage

👣 • Bathers • Picnic

Allow two to three hours – five if walking back – including an hour for pottering about and refreshments. Suggest mid-morning start. From Banjar Ambengan via Dukuh and Candi Kalebutan, then across the fields to Goa Gajah (Elephant Cave), returning on west bank of Petanu River to Banjar Ambengan. During the walk, examine the ingenious irrigation channels, side-step the fallen masonry around Goa Gajah and marvel at the unexpected galleries found along the river bank and the stone statues gracing the baths.

First, walk (or take a bemo) to *Banjar* **Ambengan** at the road junction between Ubud and **Peliatan**. Here, commencing by the *balé banjar* (more or less completing the crossroads) is a small road head-

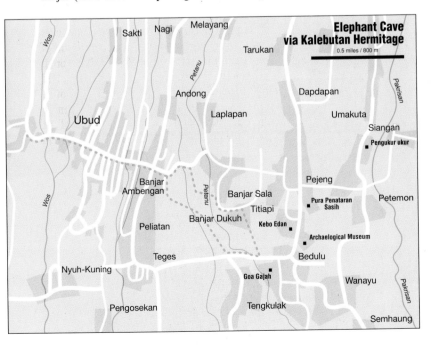

Cattle grazing

ing east, which was paved only recently and carries little traffic. Enter this road and after 100m (109yds) cross a canal to come into the open fields, away from the hubbub. It is possible from here to drive all the way to **Pejeng** but that is not our intention. Crossing a fairly deep chasm, we attain a 90 degree bend and stop, transfixed by the view.

Below, the **Petanu river** ploughs through its deep valley and a small path is plainly discerned, cutting across pasturage and leading to rock-hewn steps where the river disappears underground. Littering the length of the river-bed are colossal boulders, remnants of a collapsed irrigation tunnel, whose cleanly-sculpted lines are visible in the cliff face.

Having taken in the stupendous panorama, we proceed for about 20m (23yds) to the entrance of the little path which leads down abruptly into the valley. Chances are that smiling road-mending girls from **Klungkung** will point out the way which is obscured by a low hedge.

Remarkably, the meadow is full of edible **mushrooms** (*Agaricus campestris*) ready for picking, but that is presuming that conditions are perfect — well-watered and manured grass. Scattered cows ruminate on these emerald grounds. Why, there are even fairy rings!

Pause to examine what remains of the irrigation tunnel and consider the immense scale of the undertaking. See those massive rocks, weighing tens of tons, poised beneath a finely-wrought roof. Note how the level of the water has sunk to undermine the structure over the years. But how many years, one wonders? The whole place is honeycombed with subterranean water conduits, most of them still highly functional, as we shall note later on.

Shrieks of laughter cause us to turn and look a short distance downstream, where beautiful, naked bodies cavort and beckon

Petanu River gorge

in the churning race. Our road workers are taking an ablutionary break from the rigours of bearing and breaking paving stones.

Crossing the land bridge over the river and mounting stone steps, we look back at the recently constructed road bridge and its huge stone retaining walls, and wonder at the effort. Twenty metres (22yds) further on, the path-forks and the way leads up fairly precipitously. Passing through a pleasant wood, we presently emerge on to asphalt road.

Right to *banjar* **Dukuh**, home of wise men and *arak*. The local brew, famed for its excellent quality and potency, is not for sampling but you may buy a bottle from every household. At the next junction turn left, about 500m (545yds), to a patch of open ground and coconut plantation. We have crossed the village bounds to **Titiapi**, and before us lies the community's *kuburan* (burial ground), bordering the Kalebutan River. The *dagang* (vendor) at a nearby stall claims the *arak* of Titiapi to be the best.

Since neither *arak* nor asphalt is deemed suitable for our agenda

Candi Kalebutan

of the day, we strike off right on the path meandering through the
barrows and coconut palms, then pull up short at the edge of the
cliff overlooking the Kalebutan river. Throwing ourselves down on
the springy turf, we gaze in wonderment at the ancient rock-cut
Candi adorning the cliff wall facing us. A cave entrance yawns to
the left below, which it is possible to crawl into, but there is not
much to see, being nothing more than an obsolete irrigation tunnel.

In the foreground stands a glorious frangipani tree and on the
ridge above lie the open fields. Immediately on our right is a rough-
hewn stairway, somewhat damp and overgrown, and altogether a
bit of a scramble, leading down to a secluded cloister. An impressive
set of cells surrounds a square turfed enclosure; at one end overlooking the river and facing the sacred mountain, a looming
entrance, stepped at either side, leads to an underground apartment.

Before crossing the river over a natural arch, wander below, down
more rocky steps to a small waterspout and the tumbling stream
itself. Then, looking up at the *Candi* Kalebutan and the incredible
Gothic vaulted cavern, through which flows the watercourse and
which must have been the remnant of a prehistoric irrigation tunnel,
try to envision the setting as it was 500 years ago.

The usual complement of village belles lounges and gossips
in the cooling flow. One comely, buxom lass points
to the dark hole beneath the *candi*. '*Lelipi
gedé ada!*' – 'Big snake there!' –
she says. And they all hoot
with merriment. But
doubtless it is the lair of
the great *naga*, the serpent
that is the guardian of the
secret treasure.

Irrigation works

We continue on the path over the stream, the chasm falling away sharply to the left, surrounded by grassy banks, tangled verdure, and a lone stone shrine. Then up and right on a well-worn bund bordering the main irrigation channel. After a few metres, pause to look back across the river at the cloistered cell complex, the mysterious steps and entrance to the underground room, dripping with moss, pink orchids and ferns. What seems to be another subterranean chamber looms sombrely some distance to the right.

At a bend in the canal and path (before the concrete electric pole), we see before us the long, low line of tiled roofs, which is the *pasar* Goa Gajah – **Elephant Cave** market-place. A lone palm rears ahead, and zigzagging on the bunds, we aim for it.

Instead of running the gauntlet of clawing hawkers, we choose to adjourn to the cool, dim interior of the serenely situated **Puri Suling** restaurant. This establishment has seen better days but still provides a welcome respite from the heat and turmoil outside. We relax with our drinks, scanning the *sawa* below and the surrounding scenery.

Coconut woman? Never!

A gang of ladies labours at the rice-cutting nearby. They hail me, and one points to the tree: "*Mau kelapa?*" – "Want a coconut?" – she shouts. More roars of laughter. We may know that women never climb coconut palms. Certain activities must remain a male preserve. In any case there is refreshment enough at the shops by the road.

There is no doubt that the Goa Gajah has become what is generally known as a bit of a tourist trap. Nonetheless it is always worth a visit. Like Gunung Kawi, 'Tombs of the Kings' which we shall visit another day, the Elephant Cave dates from the 11th century and is remarkable in itself; whilst all about are ruins and fragments of similar or even greater antiquity.

Descend past mounds of fallen masonry, columns with sculpted capitals, rocky niches and secret passages, right down to the banks of the Petanu river, which sweeps by on the western side.

Swim, have a picnic, bake in the sun, and explore the galleries – presumably former quarries – which undermine the rock face on either side. Above all, marvel at the beautiful baths outside the main cave, and at the six nymphs bearing urns for waterspouts, the physiognomy of each so unlike, even the anatomies were individually inspired.

Before leaving, do not fail to inspect the gigantic *pulé* tree, next to the ticket office. Where this trifurcates, I estimate the girth to be at least 6m (20ft).

Pulé tree, Goa Gajah

Restaurant, Puri Suling

Now, if not thoroughly exhausted, I propose an easy stroll home along the western lip of the Petanu gorge. From Puri Suling/Goa Gajah walk back towards **Teges**, Ubud, perhaps 400m (¼ mile) on the road, and half-way up the hill observe a small paved road before the bridge on the left side. Proceed right on a broad track parallel to a cement-and-stone walled canal. Signs of development are already here: several large buildings have sprung up and all along the way are demarcation pegs on land sold as building sites and doubtless the road will be paved soon.

Disregarding these unwelcome signs, stroll past segregated bathing places to where the track becomes grassier and narrower between walls of *alang-alang*, passing through a dense plantation of vanilla, trained on stakes of cassia trees.

Pausing to savour views of ancient watering-places far below, and breathtaking vistas up and down the valley, we arrive suddenly at a most spectacular irrigation works. A great flow of water gushes out of one tunnel to be channelled via sluices into two further tunnels, whilst a third sluice controls the overflow. It is truly miraculous that ways have been found to convey water through these hillsides at such an elevation.

It seems that we have come to the end of the road. But the track now winds up steeply above the issuing tunnel into an expanse of *alang-alang*. At the top, bear right and continue along the western edge of the valley, through hectares and hectares of sweet-potatoes, tapioca and plantain, at times under the fretfully watching eyes of the occupants of sequestered cowsheds. To avoid instances of bolting and damage to crops, one should, on becoming aware of the animals, proceed at a normal pace, singing or whistling loudly, or smacking one's lips, at the same time taking pains not to engage the startled animals' round brown eyes.

Emerging from the arable zone, the path leads down to the valley floor, and beyond we see again the newly constructed road, bridge, and retaining walls. Instead of going all the way down and up again, bear left shortly before quitting the plantation, coming out on a narrow ridge, and, before we know it, we find ourselves on the main road once more from Ambengan to Pejeng. Wheel left, and in five minutes we are back in the bustle of Ubud.

Monkey Forest Bypass (with deviations)

Allow four to five hours (including deviations), commencing early morning or afternoon from Campuhan bridge. The walk offers a subdued look at nature's wondrous creations, the hide-and-seek flow of the river and a hermit cave and shrine behind bamboo groves. Trail skirts Penestanan Klod and Monkey Forest, crossing Wos River twice, then returning via Katik Lantang, to Penestanan Klod again, and Ubud. At Katik Lantang pay respects to an eccentric mask-dance exponent with his wonderful collection of masks.

Standing on the Campuhan bridge, note the Beggars' Bush sign on the right. A few metres further north, a small road winds around the hillside and brings us behind the wall of Blanco's garden. Wander up the road which is getting busier and turn right at the junction in the direction of Penestanan *klod*. On either side, frantic building activity proceeds apace: soon the open *sawa* will be gone. At present there exists, standing alone 200m (218yds) after the junction and on the left side, a pretty little *subak* temple – *pura dugul* or *bedugul* – which is sacred to Sri.

Leave the vehicular road here, stopping to admire the temple and its attendant trees, both deciduous. The **Red Sandalwood** (*Adenanthera pavoninus*) is with typical small *Mimosa* family leaflets, and bearing squiggly pods containing bright red seeds which are so uniform

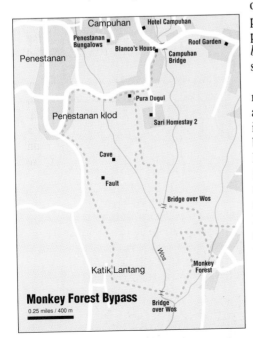

Campuhan Hotel Campuhan
Penestanan
Bungalows Blanco's House Roof Garden
Penestanan Campuhan Bridge
Pura Dugul
Penestanan klod Sari Homestay 2
Cave
Fault
Bridge over Wos
Wos
Katik Lantang Monkey Forest

Monkey Forest Bypass Bridge over Wos
0.25 miles / 400 m

Beringin tree

in size as to be used as necklace beads and 20 milligram weights.

The other, *Sterculia lanceolata*, is conspicuous at all seasons, whether naked or with new foliage, whitish to apple-green, and the old leaves turning yellow to reddish-brown. More remarkable are the fruits which consist of radiating pods. They ripen, turning from green to yellow, then through orange and vermilion to vivid scarlet, before splitting to disclose rows of shining jet-black seeds the size of peas. Sometimes enormous specimens may be seen, especially in the south and in association with temples and cemeteries.

Enough of tree-gazing, we carry on! A small concrete path leads from temple to walled villas which we pass on bund bordering the main irrigation channel. Today, the fields are newly-planted and flooded, home to a host of twittering **Wood Sandpipers** (*Tringa glareola*) and white egrets: milling above, a mass of little swiftlets.

Passing through a cool grove of palms, cloves and various fruit-trees, nestling under a huge *Albizzia* – a common member of the *Mimosa* family (known locally as *belalu*) with feathery leaves and little white pompoms, we bear left along the canal to a small dam.

Here we may jump or get our feet wet, continuing a short way through the fields to an avenue of palms, opening on our right and giving shade to a shallow gully. A flight of steps leads down inviting us to make a first detour.

Down these steps, between dappled green banks – how still and quiet it is! – we emerge in a patch of *padi* by another small temple; and following the path right and through the field, come down gently to the cleansing stream and watering-place.

Above the stream on the other side, a shrine juxtaposes a giant *beringin*, beside which looms the entrance to an irrigation tunnel – at least I think it was designed for the purpose, though everyone else will tell you that a *raksasa* scooped it out for his den.

Returning now through the *padi* to the entrance to the gully by the temple, I propose a further minor detour. A few yards in, steps carved out of the right-hand bank lead to a gap in the hedge above. Climb up and into a grassy arena bounding an area of dry cultivation. Proceed directly ahead a short way, then wheel right and pass an ancient crumbling shrine to come to the edge of a deep chasm, through which races the Penestanan stream, seemingly to disappear in the cliff face directly beneath.

A few metres further on, our progress is arrested by another precipice; yet, if we drop through the hole in the hedge at our right, trying not to cut ourselves on the clumps of pandanus planted (quite deliberately) there, we shall see that the track does in fact continue through a wooded dell and on, up some terraces. But the familiar rushing stream has mysteriously disappeared.

Pandanus

If we examine the undergrowth before us, we will see a narrow cleft but a few centimetres wide; and parting the vegetation, we are suddenly struck by the glint of reflected light and hollow gurgle of the sinuous flow, all of 40m (43½yds) below. A fascinating fault and an eerie sensation to be sure!

Having sufficiently digressed for the moment, we return by the way we came, through the gully and up the flight of steps, and out once more into the open fields. A few paces to our right is the opening to a broad, grassy track running through the centre of the *sawa*. This terminates at a canal, which having crossed we continue right on the raised bank, heading due south and away from the creeping suburbia that threatens to blot out entirely the northern horizon.

Bathing place

Keeping the irrigation stream always on our right, we arrive eventually at the tree-lined *sawa* edge, stepping from the blazing sun into the instant coolness of a coconut grove. The path leads down, past a *pondok*, on a shoulder of land formed by the confluence of Penestanan stream and Wos river – a pleasant, peaceful place where we may sit down and survey our green surrounds.

Where the Penestanan tributary flows to the right of our path, a tiny track leads to a cavernous gorge which is well worth exploring, and which is a favourite haunt of the reclusive **White-crowned Forktail** (*Enicurus leschenaultii*), notable as much for its elegant, long-tailed piebald appearance as for its piercing whistled calls. Also in the vicinity are Java Kingfisher, **Black-winged Starling** (*Sturnus melanopterus*), and the resplendent **Green Junglefowl**.

Our path winds round the shoulder to cross the Wos on a rather primitive earth-and-bamboo bridge. If this should appear at all insubstantial, it is because it is not intended to endure. Here the river ploughs deep between concave walls in what is little more than a fissure in the rock. In time of spate, the narrow rift, unable to contain the surging flow, spills over, and low-lying vegetation and makeshift bridges are swept away. The flotsam and jetsam littering the uppermost ledges and crevices are a certain indication of the latest high-water mark.

Today, there is a shaky bridge in place; without lingering on it, head up the opposing slope. A spring is channelled through *pantjoran* in the cliff-face nearby: an ideal spot to slake one's thirst, and take a cooling shower, then dry off in the sun.

Rough-hewn steps lead up through an expanse of *alang-alang* and straggly shrubs; the ideal habitat of two of Nature's more extrava-

Wos River and sawa

gantly endowed productions. The first is *Gloriosa superba*, the **Glory Lily**, which climbs through the undergrowth, putting out delicate spidery flowers, vividly coloured and variegated from pale yellow-green to all fiery red. In common with many other such bizarrely decorated members of the vegetable and animal kingdoms, the plant exhibits 'warning colours' and all parts are poisonous, especially the tubers which contain the alkaloid colchicine.

According to my manual, ingestion of this extremely poisonous substance results in numbness of the lips, tongue and throat, diarrhoea and vomiting, a burning sensation in the mouth and stomach, difficulty of breathing, convulsion and eventual death. So we admire *Gloriosa*, and without harming it, wander on.

The second curiosity is a kind of **hopper** which occurs in colonies and which is the most garishly-tinted creature I have ever seen. I do not know the name of this insect which displays all the primary colours in such violent hues that it appears to be dressed in a coat of PVC. Doubtless too, they are deadly poisonous, so we shall leave them where they are – absurdly brilliant Fauvist splotches creeping in the grass.

Through sweetly-scented flowering coffee bushes and **cocoa** – notice the similarity between the long, pointed, glossy and heavily ribbed leaves – the path continues to the small habitation, former retreat of a hermit and unexpectedly grand in such a remote situation, with its rather smart glass-panelled door and very solid foundations. No one appears to live in this oasis of tranquillity permanently now.

The hermit's cave and shrine are situated below the house and may be reached by following the track which leads through and beyond the garden. Certainly worth another detour is the cavern, which is in reality a huge hollow in the overhanging rock, and has some interesting stalactites but no bats or creepy-crawlies.

The only sounds here are the strident song of the cicada and the rush of the Wos, in its flight over boulder-strewn course to the lowlands. Higher up the slope, as the noise of the river recedes, we hear the chortle of the starlings.

A few metres before the hermit's house we may have noticed a track leading up past the cowshed on our right. This brings us once more into the fields. We are immediately struck by the difference in the stages of crop growth from one side of the river to the other.

Winding over narrow bunds to a *kubu* or little shack, then down to a lower level of *sawa*, we skirt the small wood on our right to arrive on the main path. In fact we could cut short our itinerary now, and head left up the greenish trail a short distance to Ubud.

Spider and padi field

Feeding the monkeys

It is an agreeable stroll and, in stark contrast to the parallel ridge supporting **Monkey Forest Road**, no buildings yet impinge. I suggest we carry on. Turning right, we now have two possibilities.

First Deviation: By following the ox-eye bordered path which leads down the palm-lined gully before us on the left side, we come to the picturesque spring-fed grotto, where, in less 'civilised' times, Supraba and her band of heavenly nymphs were surely wont to bathe. A very short distance beyond this is the main road.

Second Deviation: We may cut across the next expanse of *sawa* bound on three sides by ravines, and a goat-track brings us down through the tall grass into a wall of bamboo, *ficus* and *artocarpus* – the **Monkey Wood** itself. This is beyond doubt the nicest approach to an enclave which has become somewhat overpopulated of late.

Nostalgia has no place in my account, but I cannot help recalling a time before the wood (with a generous helping of tourist brochure writer's hyperbole) was transformed into a 'forest', and the only access consisted of a grassy track. No one ever thought of visiting the place, unless to bury or burn a corpse, and the resident tribe of **rhesus monkeys** or **macaques** would gibber fearfully and remain well hidden at one's approach.

Now it is a very different story, and the wretched monkeys have become hopelessly spoiled by and dependent on the endless handouts, and will not hesitate to tear the clothes off your back should they suspect that some titbit is being withheld.

I remember also the contemporary genius of the wood – black as night, with flaming blood-red eyes, brooding in the canopy above, and rending the still air with a succession of demoniacal screams. But the **Koel** (*Eudynamys scolopacea*) which is a kind of cuckoo has long since determined to haunt some more isolated grove.

For the present we are content to inspect the temple and watering places in the gorge beneath, and marvel at the immense *beringin* whose roots hold up the bridge spanning the ravine.

With clothing and possessions hopefully intact, we return from the Monkey Wood to the opening of the track which leads to the grotto. Standing with our backs to the wood, but a few paces to our left is the opening to another track which cuts down and up through the wooded gully before us.

Coming out of this, we head left (and south) on the small path running along the edge of the gully, which is rapidly developing into a grand canyon. Passing through a pretty spice garden, girt about by a brilliantly variegated croton hedge, we cross a grassy clearing past a tumbledown shed. Keep to the edge of the *sawa* – and do not be enticed into the wasteland on the left! – aim for the (south-west) corner and skirt the *alang-alang* to the avenue of palms lying obliquely ahead. Wheel left on the path beneath the sheltering palms to emerge in a sea of *alang-alang*, affording lovely vistas down the river valley. Follow down to the spring-fed stream bickering to its confluence with the Wos.

Now leap along the bedrock downstream 20m (22yds), and join the path which will take us to **Katik Lantang**. Arriving at the confluence itself, negotiate the rugged boulders to cross the main river on a narrow bamboo trestle. Then, up well-trodden bunds to the best *pantjoran* of the

Croton

lot to experience a generous hosing down.

Mightily refreshed, stroll through the fields towards Katik Lantang, which we may either enter or skirt, keeping the village on our left. Katik Lantang, a rather remote hamlet astride the pedestrian way from Penestanan to **Singakerta**, has a fine *topeng* (**mask dance**) tradition, and the current exponent **Putu Kandel**, still performs regularly in neighbouring villages. We visit him to pay our respects – a delightfully eccentric old boy, of louche (but not sinister) appearance, who will be pleased to show us his collection of masks.

It is already late, and heading up the muddy track over corrugated roots of *tjangin* trees, we bypass the village and plod through the picturesque fields towards Penestanan *klod*. The way has been widened and an asphalt road will be laid before long. From Penestanan *klod* we follow the main road back to Campuhan.

Jukut Paku

Jukut paku is the name given to fern shoots which are eaten by the Balinese with the fiery lawar (special ceremonial food). Most visitors draw the line at chewing ferns, though they will offer little resistance to partaking of either jukut nangka (stewed unripe jackfruit) or jukut ares (diced stem of plantain) with their special order of betutu (smoked, spiced duck). Why our destination should thus be named eludes me and everyone else I have spoken to, unless it is simply that abundance of ferns does grow in the place.

Allow four hours to walk there and back via Katik Lantang and **Singakerta**, returning perhaps through **Nyuh Kuning**. Walking from Campuhan to Penestanan *klod*, then south through the fields to Katik Lantang, the home of **Putu Kandel**, the mask-dance exponent.

If the way is bituminised, one may comfortably stroll on a principal parallel *sawa* bund and skirt the eastern side of the village. Similarly, a lovely grassy track leads straight through the padi from Katik

Pura Gado

Galintungan leaf

Lantang to the *pura puseh* of Singakerta. Note the extravagant gargoyles on the gate and *kulkul* tower.

From this temple, which serves also as *pura desa*, proceed west 50m (54½yds), then left at **Pura Gado**, the Temple of Commotion, which is very odd indeed. The style, with a line of stupa surmounting gate and wall, is distinctly Buddhist, while the *aling-aling*, (wall to prevent demons from entering) is decorated with weird, primitive guardians which seem quite Polynesian in character.

Continue on, past the *pura dalem*, and a wonderfully jungly *kuburan*, full of *paku* and medicinal herbs, brilliant scarlet and yellow **Parrot's Plantain** (*Heliconia*) and **Butterfly Weed** (*Asclepias*), dominated by two giant *ficus*, three or four *pulé* trees, and enormous red-barked **galintungan**, which is a species of *Bischofia*, recognised by its peculiar compound three-pronged leaves.

Down the main rutted track through Jukut Paku to the grandiosely-styled **Pura Penataran Agung** (all signs are Sanskrit incidentally) next to a large *wantilan*, where ladies dispense victuals and drinks. A track leads behind the temple to a splendid watering-place overlooking the rugged gorge of the Wos. In the *sawa* beyond, casuarinas and a row of bent frangipani fringe the glorious **Goa Raksasa**, which according to local legend was also fashioned by the monster of Campuhan, and consists of two coves flanking a *candi*.

Here, stay and meditate in a garden of **Mussaenda** (red-flag), pink hibiscus, poinciana and croton, on a springy carpet of ox-eye. We go home by following the high street through Singakerta to cross the Wos on a giddy girder bridge, turning left in Nyuh Kuning, and managing to avoid asphalt some of the way to the 'Monkey Forest', then return to Ubud on the parallel ridge.

To gain the latter we go down the great flight of steps and under the giant banyan, taking the little track directly up the slope before us and emerging into the *sawa*. Or we can take the broad track to our left, after exiting from the wood, past the natural spring-fed grotto to join the path to Ubud.

Ayung Valley

A scenic stroll which should not take above two to three hours, unless much time is spent in bathing. Best in the morning, starting from Campuhan bridge to Penestanan klod, and then Sayan at Banjar Kutuh. The trail leads into the spectacular Ayung River valley where a leisurely swim can be followed by a shower at a virgin spring. Then, heading north up-river and passing a peculiar cleft in the rock, the trail continues through narrow rice terraces before ascending the slope to Sayan Terrace. The views from here are picture-postcard perfect. Crossing the road, one returns to Campuhan via Penestanan kaja, where Hanuman, the monkey general, demands an offering along the way.

From Campuhan bridge, up the road opposite Beggars' Bush to skirt the wall running behind Blanco's studio. Go right at the junc-

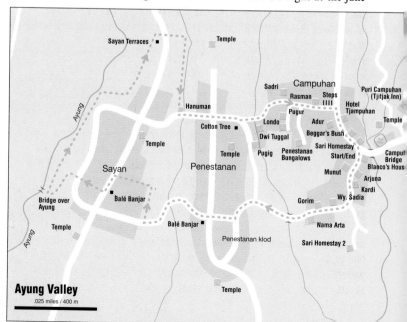

Ayung Valley

.025 miles / 400 m

Ayung valley resident

tion and continue to the southern *banjar* of Penestanan *klod*. Turn right again in the village to come to the *balé banjar*, where sits the inevitable bunch of fellows caressing their cocks. Proceed directly ahead, past the *balé* and one or two *warung*, and enter the muddy track which brings us over a small bridge and into the fields of *padi baru* (new rice).

Bearing right at a junction of canals, continue a distance of less than 100m (109yds) to cross the channel at our left on a concrete slab. The *belalu* (*Albizzia*) tree-lined track takes us past the local clinic and the village school to the main road. Here we go left, past *balé banjar* Kutuh about 100m (109yds), leaving the asphalt road on a broad lane which opens by a small lean-to on the right-hand side.

Partly cobbled, partly earth-surfaced, this lane brings us to the restful, grass-courted *Pura Nagasari,* adjacent to a square marked out for badminton and surrounded by coconut plantation. The path leads on through a great band of *alang-alang* adorning the eastern edge of the **Ayung** valley.

As we begin to make our descent, pause to survey the majestic vistas unfolding before us, the verdant palm-lined slopes on either side, overlooking the mighty Ayung itself, rushing far, far below. Partly obscured by palm fronds is the view of the aerial bamboo suspension bridge and the only access to **Bongkasa.** The nearest road-bridge lies some distance south at **Mambal.**

The track now leads down steeply through the tall grass, swerving above the swift-flowing canal and leading to another bamboo bridge – a scanty length of bamboo with or without a handrail! No matter, follow the example of other passers-by and easily wade across the canal at its widest point, with the water

'An exquisitely sculpted naiad's head'

swirling not much higher than our waists.

Go down rocky steps to the black sandy banks of the Ayung river which is the most important waterway on the island, irrigating all of Badung Regency, and much of **Gianyar.**

Whilst the flow is normally more or less turbid, do not be deterred from taking off your clothes and sliding in. Fed largely by mountain streams, the temperature of the water is always a few degrees cooler than the atmosphere, and it is most invigorating. The river sweeps leisurely round a gentle S-bend between more rapid reaches, forming a wide pool, ideal for splashing in.

Spanning the figure's centre is the bamboo bridge, partly supported on the trained limbs of trees, and if we pass beneath it, we shall see a prominent rock in the angle of the bend. Jump off the rock for a cool and surprisingly soft landing, then let yourself be carried downstream. Remember to conceal yourself modestly even if no one else appears to be about, for you are sure to be joined by the odd wayfarer.

From the shallow cliff at the edge of the wide pool, a clear rivulet tumbles; we follow this, either hugging the *sawa* edge which may

Banyan tree

be a bit boggy, or sticking to the drier bunds. Soon we attain the source, a perennial spring of powerful flow gushing from the rock-face and we sluice down at one of a series of segregated *pantjoran*.

Seek out the exquisitely sculpted naiad's head and spout nearby, where there is a solitary brick shrine, though the latter is often concealed by a luxuriant growth of moss and fern. Dry off in the sun on a well manicured lawn surrounded by greenery, flaming canna, and white-spotted *Diefenbachia*, more commonly seen in pots on patios. Marvel anew at the prodigious flow of the everlasting source, and under the spreading banyan tree, offer up a quiet thanksgiving to the shadowy spirit of this perfect place.

Then up the path above the spring, checking carefully for the entrance to the grass-cutter's track on our left which takes us along the *alang-alang* clad ridge. Should this prove too well concealed and overgrown, continue from the spring on the higher bunds at the edge of the fields to the lone coconut palm, next to which a steep path leads up to the aforementioned grass-cutter's trail. We emerge on to a dry terraced hillock with a dwelling on top, and follow the path around on either side, keeping always the Ayung on our left, the artificial channel on our right.

Passing one or two more buildings perched high on our right,

we come to a newly-constructed concrete weir and rushing fall in the irrigation channel. If anyone is still game for a swim, here is as good a spot as any for it. By mid-morning or mid-afternoon half the local populace will already be immersed. But we have soaked enough.

A path leads up the left bank into dry, grassy meadows, and bearing right takes us past another smallholding, then right again at an intersection between that compound and another, through a plantation of bananas. The mighty Ayung roars a constant reminder on our left.

A beautiful *padmasana* shrine of lichen-covered brick appears magically on an elevation at our right side, under its appointed sacred tree. Our nostrils are assailed by a waft of stale air,

Bamboo bridge, Ayung river

Sculpture of Hanuman

certain sign of subterraneous passage. Yes, there is a cave here though the path appears to be blocked by a barricade of branches on the southern side. Although our cavern is but a gaping aperture in the rock wall of the irrigation channel, it gives us an eerie sensation to creep inside, water lapping the cliff base beneath our feet. Something seems to go on here, in this dark space – a cairn and cabalistic sign scratched in the floor with remnant of a candle and a discarded offering dish.

Rice terraces cling precariously to the boulder-imbedded hillside in front of us, while the Ayung thunders in a glittering arc below. Lowering down the hill above, a file of foreign residences affords the occupants fine views.

Here did the musicologist, **Colin Macphee**, build and write *A House in Bali*, little realising that, 50 years thence, such a splendidly secluded plot would evolve into the most sought-after expatriate housing estate. Teetering on the balks, we come at last to a rough-hewn rocky ascent and walled enclosure, supposedly screening *pantjoran* from prurient public gaze. Do be very careful here: the deck is coated with slime and treacherously *blig* (slippery); and after all our exploits of the past two hours or so, we should not want to take a tumble!

Up steeply, pausing periodically to look back and savour the picture-postcard view, to join crazy-paved steps and path past various new tourist accommodation at **Sayan Terrace**, and out on to the main road. We cross straight over, continuing down a cool, shady lane bound by ancient moss-grown mud-brick walls. Coming to the main thoroughfare between Sayan and Penestanan *kaja*, we turn left, down the hill, past the cemetery and over the bridge.

Stop before stepping on to the bridge to admire the rock-carved effigies of Hanuman, the monkey general, and his simian aides, reposing by the wayside. Make an offering of flowers – not peanuts!

Entering Penestanan *kaja*, we carry straight on, past the *balé banjar*, down the path to Campuhan. One final stop to be overwhelmed by the gigantic bifurcating cotton tree (*Bombax sp.*) towering over the *pura puseh* (temple of origin). Whether naked or adorned in green mantle, array of scarlet waxy blooms, or clusters of floss-filled pods, this tree is a stunning spectacle at all seasons.

Down rocky steps and over an artificial causeway, we may wish to descend to the watering-place on our right, and inspect the nymphs sculpted from the cliff face and attending to their toilet. We traipse through the last (fast disappearing) patch of *sawa*, and down the massive flight of steps to the main road, followed perhaps by a quiet drink in a nearby tavern.

The Biggest Blooming Banyan in the World

🦶 to 🦶🦶🦶 • Bathers • Picnic • Flashlight

A good five hours allowing for a dip in the Ayung river: via Penestanan klod and Sayan, crossing Ayung to Bongkasa and heading north from Pura Puseh Banjar Sayan, Bongkasa. Stop near Pura Desa Tanggayuda to inspect the biggest ficus in the world, before continuing to a sand depot overlooking the river.

Spectacular views of new developments in Sayan, Kedewatan and of its dam before descending to an aerial bamboo bridge. A brief diversion into an eerie underground cavern with sanskrit writing on the wall. Return on the river banks past the dam-keeper's house and garden to Sayan Terrace, then back to Campuhan via Penestanan kaja.

Follow the previous itinerary into the Ayung river valley, that is, by taking the road opposite Beggars' Bush to skirt the wall behind Blanco's studio, then turn right at the junction and carry on to *banjar* **Penestanan** *klod*. Once arrived in the village, turn right and cross the square past the *balé banjar* and into the fields.

At a junction of canals, right again for a distance of 100m (109yds) only to cross the channel at your left on a concrete slab. The track leads under tall *Albizzia* trees, past the village clinic and school,

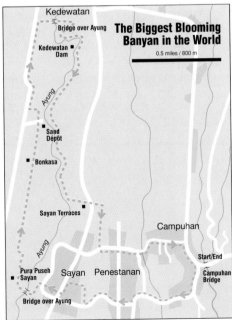

The Biggest Blooming Banyan in the World

0.5 miles / 800 m

Kedewatan
Bridge over Ayung
Kedewatan Dam
Ayung
Sand Dépôt
Bonkasa
Sayan Terraces
Campuhan
Ayung
Pura Puseh Sayan
Sayan   Penestanan
Start/End
Campuhan Bridge
Bridge over Ayung

Heavy rain

The angklung band played on!

Once I had the pleasure of accompanying the marching *angklung* orchestra of Penestanan to a ceremony here. It had been raining heavily before the procession started out, and it was no easy matter transporting the heavy gongs across raging rapids and up and down slithery slopes, but the band kept playing all the way! How easy it had been for me, unencumbered by anything more than a pair of binoculars.

to the main road in **Sayan** at *balé banjar* **Kutuh**.

A hundred metres (109yds) down the road, a small track leads to the right beside a lean-to and this happens to be the principal pedestrian thorough-fare to **Bongkasa**.

Passing the beautifully situated *pura Nagasari*, the trail descends through *alang-alang* to a bamboo bridge over a major irrigation canal. From here the trail continues down to the Ayung river itself.

Either swim across the river or clamber over the bridge, then climb to the irrigation channel which follow north for about 100m (109yds). The path leads up into a wall of vegetation which is someone's back-garden. Instead of entering the latter, proceed north on the obvious track above the canal which brings us to the forecourt of a temple.

There is no sign in any language to tell us that this is the *pura puseh* of *banjar* Sayan, Bongkasa, or that '*It is Forbidden to Enter Menstruating Women*'. No one needs to be told such things here. What an enchanting place; beautifully wrought and ornamented brick buildings, surrounded by spacious lawn.

North of the temple, stone steps lead down to a well-shaded track

Ayung river valley

Sand-loading depots

into *banjar* **Tanggayuda**. It is confusing that some of the 11 *banjar* of **Bongkasa** should bear the same names as those of **Kedewatan** across the river. There is a relative absence of activity over here, accentuating the extraordinary stillness of the place. The mainly mud-brick dwellings are set in exceptionally large and lush gardens. Here, land is not at such a premium.

Continue more or less straight, bearing left at intervals, since many of the wider, rutted tracks tend to lead to sand-loading depots at the valley's edge. We may also follow the recently-installed line of power pylons. Soon we come to another splendid temple with no name. Should we have difficulty in finding our way, enquire the direction to *pura desa* Tanggayuda. The rustic sanctuary prepares us for the tree which is to follow.

What appears to be a large wooded area situated beyond the temple is the banyan tree that has become a forest. A central bole has long since been replaced by adventitious growth which extends over about an hectare. Marvel in silence at the design of aerial filaments and great embrangled limbs, supporting a host of epiphytes as well as massy crown. And an army of squirrels, birds, and lizards.

Nearby is the village school, and beyond that a road which is partly asphalted, and along which the occasional motorcycle, truck, and old-fashioned bemo pass. We could continue that way but that means missing the spectacle of sand collection. So proceed north from the banyan on another broad track which terminates at the main depot.

A sensible sign declares: '*Harga Pasir Rp. 5,000*' – 'Price of Sand 5,000 Rupiah' (per cubic metre) – which seems quite reasonable. Positioned along the lip of the gorge is a battery of primitive, hand-operated pulleys hauling buckets of sand from the river 80m (250ft) below. A team of husky ladies, permanently immersed, ducks down

to scoop up the alluvial deposit from the river-bed.

A surprising number still stagger up the slope, heavy containers balanced on heads. Hard work – either way! We may short-cut our journey now, descending to cross the rickety trestle-bridge used by the sand-bearers, though we should forfeit further opportunities of certain excitement and sensational views.

Back along the track to an S-bend from which a narrow path leads north again that connects with the main patchy asphalt road. This brings us to the very edge of the valley where we hear the swelling roar of the cascade at Kedewatan dam.

Now we can discern the dam beneath us, arced curtain of the fall, and seething white cauldron below. Everywhere else is an unrelieved green though there appear to be many newly-thatched roofs scattered through the rim of vegetation opposite.

A hundred metres (109yds) past the next S-bend in our road, a small stall is located on the left side. A few metres further on and opposite is the entrance to the narrow track which takes us down to what I believe is now the only bridge between here and **Payangan**, a few miles to the north. Since there is no sign and the way so unremarkable, and as stalls and other markers may often be removed, it is expedient to know the Indonesian word for bridge – *jembatan* (or in Balinese *titi*).

We hasten down the muddy, claustrophobic track to emerge suddenly in the open; a dazzling vista of the river valley unfolding at our feet. But there is better yet to come.

A slight, flat-topped eminence arises before us which we mount for unrivalled views of the valley on either side. The incredible scale of new building developments atop the opposing slope may now be clearly seen; and of course one can have no real conception of its extent when viewed either from below or above on the eastern side. True, the buildings for the most part are well designed and made from local materials, but still they are bound to obtrude, inasmuch as they appear where none appeared before.

Your Balinese dwellings remain well tucked away behind a communal curtain of green. We take a last, lingering look at Nature's extravagant productions reflecting on the contrasting types of extrinsic growth that have come under our scrutiny today.

From here the way down is fairly straightforward but for the adventurous spirit one deviation is proposed. It has to be admitted that none but your most ardent speleologist (cave enthusiast) may be tempted to undertake it.

Make sure that you are following in my steps down the original trail which leads to the right side of and below the little hillock. At a point about half way down, a small track leads off to the left. Not far down this, you will see a peculiar hollow or broad fault developing on the right side. The upper level or terrace of the cliff-walled amphitheatre is easily gained by a narrow grassy ledge leading down from our path.

Striding across the arena, the ground suddenly falls away in a steep scree slope, obstructed usually by fallen trees – deliberately obstructed I should think. Scrambling down, over and around the various obstacles, one approaches the yawning cavern mouth where

the last bit is a bit tricky and slippery owing to subsidence of the accumulated rubble.

Pause a moment before we slide in, and inspect the vast gloomy interior, relieved in the background by a beam of light from a vertical shaft cut through the cavern roof. The whole is evidently chiselled out by the hand of man, but when? – and for what possible purpose? Easing ourselves in, we proceed along the huge passage, splashing through ankle-deep water, to where the ray of light streams from the roof, striking a flat-surfaced rock pedestal.

Upon this convenient table I once placed a vital clue in a treasure hunt which I organised for the runners of Hash House Harriers. Not many ventured to retrieve it! Perhaps the container

Beringin tree

Hewn in the living rock

is still there. Whatever else may be there, I am unable to tell you; you will have to find out for yourself.

Returning to the light of day and the main trail, note a perfectly turfed enclave on your left side where the path dips down between rock walls. A lovely *padmasana* shrine provides a seat for visiting deities. It appears to have been there forever but a date is etched into the stone – 1969 – a good vintage year! In the cliff face behind are inscribed a series of sanskrit or *kawi* hierographs which must be of considerable antiquity. Or are they ...?

Here comes the bridge, an astonishing contraption of bamboo poles and palm cross-ties, suspended on coat-hanger wire some 20m (64ft) above the swirling flood. Some of the poles look rather suspect: others appear to have disintegrated entirely. Try not to look down. Periodic repairs are called for and these are financed by local *banjar* funds. A small toll may be exacted by a *banjar* appointee on the Bongkasa side. Should this be the case, then please give generously!

Should you feel sufficiently exerted continue up directly to the road and catch a bemo back to Ubud. A nicer way to go home is to turn right where our path joins the flight of cement steps leading down to the Kedewatan dam.

Descend once more to near the level of the river, all the way on even steps and along carefully raked gravel paths, lined with multi-coloured croton and a variety of flowering shrubs. Our entire route is one enormous and endless herbaceous border. Coming to the dam itself, pause to gaze down at the thunderous fall and churning mass below, and muse on the prospect of floating over the barrage in a dinghy. It has been done; and the river below is a great challenge.

Hash House Harriers

Cave entrance

Note the irrigation canal that originates from the main sluice gate. In a pretty garden with a lily-pond stands the dam-keeper's house and office. Alongside is the derelict Dutch-style building that formerly housed the dam-keeper's family. One feels that it ought to be refurbished. What a marvellous place to reside with only the sound of water crashing over the weir.

Our path leads past the house, through floral borders beside the canal, and continues on a plane above the river. More elaborate sluices are encountered on the way; sometimes the canal vanishes underground or is covered with a concrete casing, presumably to prevent blockage by landslides. And we wonder anew at all this precision, and the priority given to distributing the life-giving flow.

Gradually the path rises, skirting a smallholding and traversing narrow rice terraces, to climb rocky steps to another gushing spring. Superb space and timing for a bath. Go along the ledge and on to familiar ground at the foot of Sayan Terrace. We mount to the asphalt road and cross directly over, returning via Penestanan *kaja,* past the *pura puseh* and its fantastic cotton-tree, and through the fields to the huge steps leading down to the main road of Ubud.

Cotton tree

Monkey Forest

Not to be confused with Ubud's misnomer, this grove of giant trees and cavern is well worth a visit. From Campuhan bridge allow a minimum of six hours to walk there and back. The name of the place is Sangeh, and you will find it on every tourist map.

Retrace itinerary *The Biggest Blooming Banyan In The World* to the *pura puseh Banjar Sayan.* From the temple proceed due west on a tiny hedged path to main road. Turn left, continuing past asphalt and dirt road junction another 300m (327yds) on asphalt to the next 90 degree bend, then right to the end of the dirt road. A muddy track leads to a delightful watering place, with cubicles for boys and girls, then across a small stream with more *pantjoran,* and out to the edge of a panoramic expanse of rolling *sawa.*

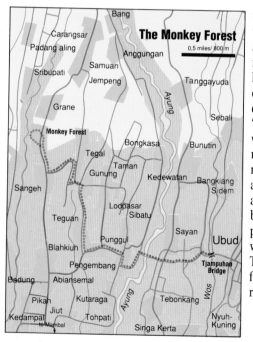

From here it is built up most of the way, as we pass through various *banjar* of *desa* **Taman**, nearly (but not) always heading in a westerly direction. When in doubt, question anyone '*Jalan* Sangeh?' and you will be pointed in the right direction. The last mile and a half is now asphalted, and the lake at **Taman Mumbul**, just before Sangeh, while still picturesque, is choked with **Water Hyacinth**. The baths, always refreshing, are slightly redolent of duckweed.

On attaining the high-

Taman Mumbul

way in Sangeh, the great wall of **Dipterocarpus trees** looms quarter of a mile to the north. To avoid the gauntlet of souvenir-sellers, wander past the wood and approach it from the rear. Enter anywhere on a carpet of dead leaves, and commune with the nearest giant. Here are some of the most magnificent trees I have ever seen, unlimbed boles dead straight for well over 30m (100ft). It is easy to ignore the monkeys.

Behind the wood, a path leads through the *sawa* to a clove plantation and substantial house, poised on the brink of an abysmal chasm. Steps lead down to a pump-well at the very bottom, and the spring which gushes from the cliff-face at one end disappears into a swallow-hole at the other.

The entrance is silted up as a result of a recent massive landslip, but it is still possible to crawl in along the stream bed. After a few metres, one finds oneself inside a monstrous cavern, and very soon one's eyes become accustomed to the wall of blackness, which gradually diminishes as a bend in the chamber is rounded, and daylight is perceived flooding through the mouth.

Treading with lighter step along the stream bed or perfectly good path above it, and admiring the amazing rock formation about us, we emerge under the sun. Nothing on earth will prevent us from plunging into the glorious river sparkling at our feet. This is gamely followed by climbing up another convenient flight of steps to the house and a kiosk serving icy drinks. Of course we could have chosen to descend these steps first, but that would have spoilt half the fun of it. We go back to Ubud the way we came.

Water Hyacinth

91

Pala leaf and seed

Lychee Boulevard

🦶🦶🦶 • Bathers

If we walk the whole way, with the odd dip and diversion, and take time off for tree-gazing and bird-watching, it will take us all day. As in the Biggest Blooming Banyan itinerary, begin by taking the road behind Blanco's studio, then turning right at the junction to banjar Penestanan klod. At the village turn right and cross the square past the balé banjar and into the fields.

Coming to a junction of canals, turn right again a short distance to cross the channel on your left on a concrete slab. Follow the track shaded by *Albizzia* trees, past the village clinic and school to the main road in Sayan at *balé banjar* Kutuh. A hundred metres (109yds) down the road, a small track leads to the right beside a lean-to which is the main walkway to Bongkasa.

Continue on the Bongkasa side of the Ayung river, heading north through **Banjar Karang Dalem**. *Karang dalem* means steep cliff, and

Dipterocarp forest

a track near the *pura dalem* takes you to the brink of a dizzy cliff on a bend of the river, with an equally dizzy precipice on the opposite left bank. With any luck you will see here the **Spotted Kestrel** (*Falco moluccensis*), which nests on inaccessible rock ledges nearby, and not a sign of any human habitation.

Continue north, emerging into the first stretch of *sawa*, and pass through **Anggungan**, before reaching **Bang**, whence a rough path descends steeply to the only bridge spanning the Ayung for miles in either direction. I have walked this way only three times, and on the first two occasions I noticed rows of *sungga* – sharp bamboo spikes – planted at intervals along the track. These are sometimes found on seldom-trodden paths in out-of-the-way places, and are a potent deterrent to trespassers, which may be taken to mean anyone from outside these remote communities.

So proceed cautiously on the downhill slope. A tumble-down shack in the middle of nowhere houses the toll-gatherer, and I entreat you to empty your pockets unproudly if you wish to pass. This bridge, for all its fearsome appearance, is worth preserving. Approached on either side by a steep rock-hewn stairway, it spans the most majestic canyon in the Ayung's foaming course.

We climb up through a lovely wood of teak trees in which monkeys gibber anxiously and remain out of sight. Then – lo and behold! – a Chinese burial ground perched on the pinnacle. Of all God's acres I have come across, this must be the most dramatically situated. A little **Pied Bushchat** (*Saxicola caprata*) stands atop a gaudily-decorated mausoleum; his dowdier wife on another glittering tomb nearby. Cows munch happily between the slabs. What a perfect resting place.

Then out, through a long avenue of palms in a shimmering expanse of fields. There is only one main path which brings us eventually up a sidelane into **Paya-ngan**. If the fruit market is in full swing and lychees are in season, we should make the most of our opportunity, assuming we have not spent all our money. At intervals the shapely trees with dark green crowns adorn the wayside.

Stuffed with lychees, we may elect to take a bemo directly home. Better to walk east and south via **Klusa** and **Keliki**, coming back to Campuhan directly on the ridge (see The Ridge itinerary).

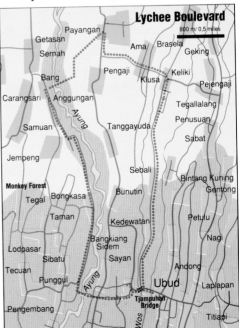

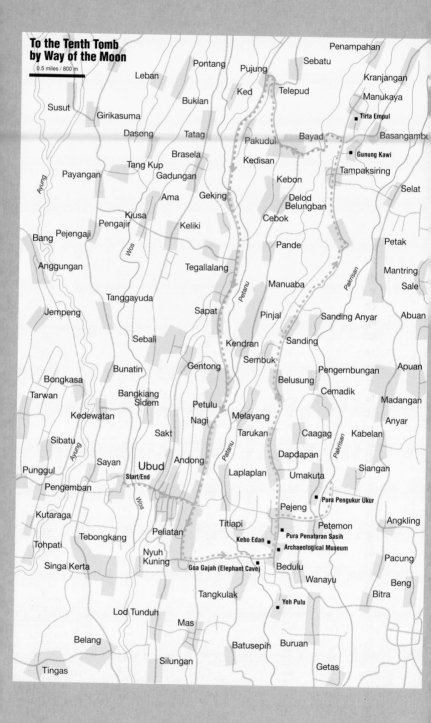

To the Tenth Tomb by Way of the Moon

0.5 miles / 800 m

Penampahan
Sebatu
Pontang
Pujung
Leban
Ked
Telepud
Kranjangan
Manukaya
Susut
Bukian
Girikasuma
Tirta Empul
Dasong
Tatag
Pakudui
Bayad
Basangambu
Brasela
Kedisan
Gunung Kawi
Tang Kup
Payangan
Gadungan
Kebon
Tampaksiring
Ama
Geking
Delod
Belungban
Selat
Kiusa
Keliki
Cebok
Pengajir
Bang
Pejengaji
Wos
Pande
Petak
Anggungan
Tegallalang
Mantring
Sale
Tanggayuda
Petanu
Manuaba
Pakrisan
Jempeng
Sapat
Pinjal
Sanding Anyar
Abuan
Sebali
Kendran
Sanding
Bunatin
Gentong
Sembuk
Pengernbungan
Apuan
Bongkasa
Bangkiang
Sidem
Belusung
Cemadik
Madangan
Tarwan
Petulu
Kedewatan
Nagi
Melayang
Caagag
Kabelan
Anyar
Sibatu
Sakt
Tarukan
Pakrisan
Ayung
Sayan
Andong
Petanu
Dapdapan
Siangan
Punggul
Ubud
Laplaplan
Umakuta
Pengemban
Start/End
Wos
Pejeng
Pura Pengukur Ukur
Angkling
Kutaraga
Titiapi
Petemon
Tebongkang
Peliatan
Pura Penataran Sasih
Tohpati
Kebo Edan
Archaeological Museum
Pacung
Nyuh
Kuning
Singa Kerta
Goa Gajah (Elephant Cave)
Bedulu
Beng
Wanayu
Bitra
Tangkulak
Yeh Pulu
Lod Tunduh
Mas
Belang
Batusepih
Buruan
Tingas
Silungan
Getas

To The Tenth Tomb by Way of The Moon

**👣 • 👣👣 (if not motoring) • Bathers •
Picnic • Sarong • Flashlight**

A morning, or preferably afternoon, outing calling for transport.
One may walk on asphalt from Ubud at banjar Ambengan via
Titiapi to Pejeng, where the Moon and Goa Garba are found.
Then one can walk north, following the course of the Pakrisan
River, all the way to Gunung Kawi and the Tenth Tomb in
Tampaksiring. If walking, allow all day — one-way!

Our main aim is to avoid asphalt today, so we shall hire a motorcar, and venture somewhat further afield. There will be rambling
enough to compensate for the enforced ride.

From Ubud, we drive to Pejeng via Peliatan and **Bedulu** where
we may inspect Goa Gajah, the Elephant Cave, if we have not yet
had occasion to walk there (see the *Elephant Cave* itinerary).

In Pejeng, a prominent sign on the right opposite the football
field announces our arrival at **Pura Penataran Sasih** – Temple of
the Great Hall of the Moon. Entering the outer gate, flanked by a

Goa Garba

Morning Glory

pair of huge guardian *gajah*, we will be invited to put on sashes and sarongs by courteous and attentive custodians. Few tourists come here.

What immediately impresses us other than the airy spaciousness and exquisite architecture, is the lovely garden. Soft lawn dotted with flowering trees and shrubs – Pagoda flowers and orchids, red and orange **Poinciana** (yellow too), Champak and Mussaenda (*M. glabra*) with white sepals, and Frangipani dripping blossoms all about. Most fragrant of all, **Ylang-ylang**, known by the Balinese name *sandat* (*Cananga odorata*), its subtle, musky perfume best appreciated first thing in the morning, and in the hour before dusk.

The amazing '**Moon**' is enshrined within the inner court. A unique bronze drum of prodigious size and unknown provenance, it is thought to belong to some forgotten Indonesian bronze age, not unrelated to the **Dông-Zon** culture of Annam (now Vietnam) which swept through Asia around 2,500 years ago, and probably introduced rice cultivation to the Indonesian archipelago.

Given that old bronze drum castings have been found in Bali, it is by no means inconceivable that the thing was made here. The entire surface is decorated in bas-relief with intricate designs which are more characteristically Indo-nesian than Chinese, including the highly stylised faces of the sides. Binoculars are required to examine the detail for the drum is a much revered object, and no one is allowed to go near it.

Aside from the great attraction of the *balé Sasih*, with its finely sculpted **Bedawang** (the Cosmic Turtle) base and *idjuk* roof (which distinction it shares only with the *balé agung*), the Pura Penataran Sasih boasts also an intriguing collection of statuary, some of it dating from very early times. In addition to several well-preserved *linga* and figures of **Ganesa**, the elephant-headed god of foresight, there are some splen-did pieces which seem to owe much to Khmer influence; still others which are strangely

Pakrisan River valley

Ptolemaic in appearance.

Admiring the condition and grand scale of the various brick and *paras* buildings, and praying that the grass carpet beneath them will not be replaced by paving, we hand back our finery to the attendants, at the same time making a handsome contribution to the general upkeep of the place.

It is but a short distance by car to the crossroads in Pejeng, where we turn right. We are going to visit the little-known **Goa Garba.** The road winds through *banjar* **Panglan**, and not deviating from the bitumen, we turn left at the next junction towards **Sawagunung**. Coming out of the final bend past the village compounds, we enter a straight stretch for several hundred metres, a high bank on our left, the village school and **Pura Pengukur Ukuran** (clearly signed) a short way up on our right. Before the

Sasih the Moon Drum

Local legend has it that the *Sasih* is a *subang* (ear-plug) of either **Dewi Ratih**, the moon goddess, or our old friend Kbo Iwa, the man-eating giant, who left an indelible impression on both the landscape and its inhabitants.

Another story of zestful Balinese flavour tells us that the *Sasih* is indeed the moon, which once fell from the night-sky, becoming lodged in the branches of a tree. The glare it gave off was so terrific that it prevented some thieves from going about their illicit business. One member of the gang then climbed the tree and proceeded to urinate on the source of all-revealing light in order to extinguish it. Whereupon the moon exploded, putting paid to the fellow's matrimonial prospects, and falling to the ground in the form of the drum we see now, which also accounts for the piece missing from the underside.

Goa Garba

school a track leads down into the heavenly **Pakrisan River valley**.

When I last visited there, I was aghast to see that a really nasty cement pylon had been erected at the entrance. What this presages I cannot say, but there is no doubt that more visitors have been coming to this out-of-the-way spot since the road was paved a few years ago. We leave the car by the roadside and walk.

We wander down past the waving *alang-alang*, the valley opening up before us, the crystal-clear water weaving a welcome spell below. With awesome suddenness, the great gate looms above its pile of monolithic steps. The wall of the citadel is the rock face; and higher up are vestiges of other walls, walkways and watering-places. At the base of the cliff are cells with unusually moulded pediments, and containing fragments of statuary and other carved *objets*. Before we explore, I suggest that we go down to the glittering river and plunge in. The water is unbelievably cool and refreshing – to the first tentative toeing, actually cold!

There are some peculiar niches and cavities in the rock platform nearby. Further upstream are caves, including one large semicircular aperture on the right side which harbours at its entrance a huge slab of toppled masonry, indented in the shape of the letter B. Just before it

Stonework at Pura Pengukur Ukuran

are some interesting rock-cut friezes of indeterminate design and age. This, I was told by a local farmer who led me to the place, is the *goa* of Goa Garba. But I am not so sure.

Returning to the ruin, we mount the monstrous steps, formed of individual boulders of river-worn igneous rock, as opposed to hand-worked volcanic tuff. These must be megalithic; they appear to ante-date everything else here, not to say all the other ancient monuments I have seen.

An old boy told me a rather garbled tale of an insatiable giant who invaded the neighbourhood and enslaved its populace. Having well-nigh exhausted their resources, it was resolved to entertain the unwanted guest to one lavish final feast, at which he ate so hugely and drank such copious quantities of wine, that he could scarcely crawl back to his cave. Once inside, he fell into a deep sleep which lasted several days, during which time the villagers were able to con-struct a wall solid enough to con-tain him, and there he remains to this day.

Pura Pengukur Ukuran

The steps are undeniably steep. We haul ourselves through the magnificent archway, then proceed along the terrace and down more manage-able steps to a series of ancient watering-places that culminate in an immense, square sunken bath let into the cliff. Behind the bath is a wall of such meticulously pre-cise construction that no interstice exists between its stone layers. It is very curious, this wall.

At the opposite end of the bath various blocks of masonry are arranged in a roughly rectangular pattern. Why are they so ordered? The central slab covers a shaft, with steps leading down into a tunnel, which runs in both directions behind the cliff face. A few metres in, on either side, the passage is obstructed by a wall of earth and rubble.

But we must press on; the **Tenth Tomb** still awaits. Marvelling at the enormous trees – *Sterculia* or *Alstonia*? – which overlook the monument, we continue up the giant's causeway. At the top, a small path leads to a side-gate of the temple, **Pura Pengukur Ukur**. *Ukur* is Balinese for size or measure, and the story goes that it was orig-inally planned to build the mother temple of all Bali here; but in the event, the size of the site was deemed insufficient, and so Bali's most important sanctuary was established at **Besakih** instead.

We may not enter (without the correct dress), but at least we may steal a peep through the gate at wonderfully decorated shrines and pavilions. One huge, pyramidic *padmasana* is the throne of **Surya**,

the sun god, nearest to us, its lower tiers adorned with splendid *linga*, borne on the back of *Bedawang* the turtle who supports the foundations of the world. But something drastic has occurred since my last visit. The entire inner court has been concreted.

Now, there is a legend that somewhere in the vicinity is concealed the entrance (or one of the entrances) to the passage that leads under the sea to the island of **Nusa Penida**. I have heard tell of a ceremony in the Pura Pengukur Ukur in which the priest steps into a hole in the ground and is not seen again for three days; and supposedly, during that time, he journeys underground and under the **Badung Strait** to emerge in Penida from the Goa Putri, the Lady's Cave, at **Karangsari**. Another entrance is said to be at the famous Bat Cave, **Goa Lawa**, not far from **Kusamba**.

Far-fetched, you may think! When you have been to *Goa Garba*, to *Goa Lawa* and *Goa Putri*, and made a thorough study of the topography, everything becomes plausible. There may be more to myth than permeates the mind, and more to *Goa Garba* than meets the eye. *Garba*, it should be explained, is a word from the old poetic *kawi* tongue, which may literally be translated as the 'belly of the world' or 'bowels of the earth'.

We pass through the forecourt on a carpet of blossoms shed by a vast champak tree and walk back to the car.

Outside Pejeng *kaja*, the road winds down sharply to pass over a steep gorge where we stop for a moment to lean over the parapet and peer into the dreamy green depths. The thought that the entrance to the secret passage might have inadvertently been sealed by the concrete flooring of the templed court gives cause to my distress.

As the air becomes appreciably cooler so the vegetation assumes a lusher aspect. In **Tampaksiring**, a sign directs us to **Gunung Kawi.** In recent years, the touristic potential of the 'Kings' Tombs' has begun to be realised. Since there are several hundred steps to go down and up, it is by no means as popular as the nearby **Tirta Empul** temple with its sacred baths and spring.

There are a carpark and ticket-office, and the usual horde of persistent shopkeepers. However, nothing can detract from our pleasure at the astonishing spectacle that awaits us. Descending the steps, past irrigation channels crammed with bathers, we arrive at a point perhaps a third of the way down where an open terrace on our right affords a splendid view of the monumental complex.

The Pakrisan rushes loudly along the floor of its stupendous valley. All the hillside above is holed with coves or excavated cells, while to our left, through the pinkish tips of clove trees, we glimpse five rock-hewn-*candi* of awesome proportions.

We could stand here all day surveying this incredible setting but there is much that calls for a closer inspection. Through the tremendous stone gate, hemmed in by stone walls, our path leads down to the river. If we cross over on the footbridge, we shall be required to wear temple dress for we shall not want to miss the most elaborate set of coves and cloisters located within the temple precincts.

Immediately to our left is the path leading to the first group of four gigantic *candi*. Variously

I tell you another bird story of the Sunda Whistling Thrush

In this selfsame cooling stream some years ago, a sudden movement caught my attention. There, perched on a boulder in mid-stream, barely five metres away, was one of the most beautiful birds I had seen. Obviously a kind of thrush, the bird was a rich, dark purplish-blue, which gave off a metallic sheen in the sunlight. It stood there rather lopsidedly, glaring at me for fully five seconds, then shot off downstream with a loud screech; and only then did I realise that it had a gammy leg, which it trailed awkwardly in flight.

I had never seen this bird before, but I concluded that it must be a **Sunda Whistling Thrush** (*Myophonus glaucinus*), a shy, uncommon bird of the wild, which is known only from the **Greater Sundas**, i.e. Borneo, Java and Sumatra, and Bali. I suspect that at one time it had been trapped and managed to escape, finally finding sanctuary at *Gunung Kawi*, which may be translated as 'Mountain of Antiquity' or 'Rock of Ages'.

Gunung Kawi is a place I visit frequently, and over the course of the following two years or so, I came to be well acquainted with my friend with the maimed leg, and he came to recognise me. Usually I would find him by the stream where there was abundance of the snails on which he fed. There were times when he was unaccountably absent, but I knew I should discover him somewhere in the vicinity, and I made it a point never to return home without first paying my respects.

I remember the acute feeling of desolation I experienced that first time when he failed to appear by the stream. I entered the temple and wandered behind the cloistered walls of the hermitage. As I was passing the last cell before re-entering the quadrangle, suddenly, with a tremendous screech, the thrush erupted from the black alcove and shot through the gate towards the stream. Thereafter, I would often surprise my solitary friend in one or other of the rocky cavities. At times, it was almost as if we were playing a game of hide-and-seek.

Then I had to go abroad for a few months. On my return, almost the first thing I did was to drive to Tampaksiring. I went directly down the steps and to the water's edge. Not a sign, anywhere. I made a search of the cloisters and caves inside as well as outside the temple. Again I drew a blank. Perhaps my lonely bird had decided to take up residence elsewhere.

I was preparing to leave, when I spied the *pemangku*, priest of the temple, approaching. I hailed him, and following an exchange of civilities, I asked if he remembered the blue bird with the gammy leg. Of course, he knew the bird well, he said – then came a long pause – well? – well, it had been shot!

Shot! What on earth for? Who could have done such a heinous thing? Poor crippled fugitive. In this sacred enclave. A young visitor from afar, apparently: from an influential family. No one could stop him. And that, I grieve to say, was the end of my lame and lovely Sunda Whistling Thrush.

attributed to the 11th century kings, **Erlangga** (or his brother who ruled Bali in his name) and **Anak Wungsu**, the monuments were not actually discovered until 1920, or at least were unknown to anyone but the local farmers.

Possibly the four 'tombs' before us commemorate favourite concubines of the king, while the five on the other side of the river were built for his queen and kinsmen. No one really knows. It is not even certain that a king is buried here. There is, however, another resting place, set apart perhaps for one whose person was held sacred, if not semi-divine. It is this secluded place, invisible from the main complex and seldom visited by anyone, that is known as the Tenth Tomb.

Meanwhile, before we explore the gloomy recesses secreted in the temple across the water, I suggest that we follow the little path to the side of the cliff, down to the river, and cleanse ourselves in the cooling stream.

One is not exactly encouraged to visit the **Tenth Tomb**. The path is slippery and steep, and, in any case, it is not such a grand and imposing spectacle. Neither do I recommend that everyone should go there. But if you are game, where the dwindling stone wall comes to an end on the steps, we may scramble down and strike off along the obviously worn edge of the *sawa*.

Past a bathing place, rough steps lead down, and rounding a bend, the stone entrance-gate looms before us. The interior passage is mossy and dank, and coming out of it, the first niches, partly collapsed, appear in the rock. Crossing a small stream, where **White-crowned Forktails** are nearly always present, whistling shrilly, the

Traditional mudbrick thatched huts

perfect crescent of the cliff now confronts us, a central *candi* flanked by coves ranged the entire length on either side.

To describe the plain, rustic beauty and serenity of this hallowed place, devotedly crafted to preserve the memory of warrior king or spiritual leader – now weathered and transformed by the natural accretions of a millennium – to attempt to describe it, is to fly in the face of objectivity. One has to experience it for oneself. We will linger here a while and let the spirit of the Tenth Tomb touch and moderate us, as the green growth softens the austere and immemorial stone.

We can go back the way we came, but I am for continuing through the second gate, and up the steep and normally muddy track to narrow rice terraces suspended in space. More cells are visible in the cliff to our left. Mind your step! The path narrows and passes over the edge of an abyss. Vertigo sufferers (and everyone else for that matter) should climb the specially excavated steps to the highest level of *sawa*, avoiding the chasm altogether.

Up, and over three more watercourses, each bridged, before we enter the village. Turn right for the final stretch between lovely, crumbling, moss-clad, mud walls, with here and there a fascinating glimpse of traditional mud-brick, thatched huts within; and before we know it, we are back at the car.

We drive home via Pujung, so turn right on the main road, and then left at the crossroads a little further on. The bridge over the river gorge just before **Bayad** makes the one we stopped at on the way up from Pejeng seem like child's play. Park in the middle, and feel distinctly uncomfortable, floating 120m (394ft) up in the air.

Turn right at the next road junction, past the Pura Ulun Sui of Bayad, and to a vantage ground commanding amazing views over a vast area right up to the mountain range. Behind us an ocean of *padi Bali*. One or two huts and stalls have sprung up which were not there before. The *orang turis* are coming!

Before arriving in Pujung, a turning on our right leads to **Sebatu**, an ancient village with interesting architecture and an exceptional *gong*; also some very fine baths and *pantjoran* at a place known also as **Gunung Kawi**. If we have time, it would be unwise not to take a bath here. From Pujung a wonderfully scenic drive straight back to Ubud, trying hard to ignore the multitude of new shops springing up along the way; at the same time resolving to return to the Petanu and Pakrisan river valleys, and the strip of land between, with their many charming relics of antiquity. But will we ever have time to see them all?

Right, temple decorations

Glossary

ada	have, is. There is, there are
agung	great and mighty
air minum	drinking water
air	water
alang alang	coarse grass used for thatching
asli	real, original, authentic
angklung	portable orchestra
arak	distilled palm toddy
attap	roofing of palm-frond
bahasa	language, bahasa Indonesia
balé banjar	village ward meeting hall
balé	pavilion
barong	powerfully magic mythical beast
baru	new
bedawang	cosmic world turtle
blig (belig)	slippery
bukit	hill
campuran	mixture
candi	rock-carved stupa, burial tower
dagang	hawker, street vendor
dalem	deep, steep
desa	village
dewi	goddess
gajah	elephant
ganesa	elephant god, god of foresight
gedé	big
goa	cave, any rock excavation
gong	orchestra
gula	granulated sugar
gunung	hill, mountain
hidjo (hijau)	green
idjuk (ijuk)	fibre of sugar palm
jagung	corn, maize
jalan jalan	walking, rambling
jalan	road
jembatan	bridge
kaja	north, to the mountains
kangin	east, right
kantor	office
karang	rock, cliff, reef
kau	west, left
kawi	the ancient language, poetry
kepeng	chinese cash
klod (kelod)	south, to the sea
kopi	coffee
kubu	small shack

kuburan	burial ground
kulkul	alarm drum, tomtom
linga	stone phallus
lukisan	painting
makan	eat
mekiis/melasti	ritual ablution
minum	drink
orang biasa	ordinary man, man-in-the-street
orang	man, person
orang turis	tourist
padi asli	original rice
padi baru	new (high-yield) rice
padi	rice-field, growing rice
paku	fern
pantjoran	water spout
paras	soft volcanic rock, tuff
pasar	market-place
pemangku	temple priest
penyor	decorated bamboo pole
pesedahan	subak office of government administrator
pondok	cabin
pura bedugul (dugul)	subak temple
pura beji	river temple
pura dalem	temple of the dead
pura desa	village temple
pura penataran	royal temple
pura puseh	temple of origin, navel temple
pura	temple
pura ulun sui	subak temple
pura ulun tjarik	subak temple
puri	palace
rangda	witch
raksasa	demon
redjang	a stately temple dance
sanga limas/tjutjuk	subak shrines
sari	blossom
sarong	length of batik cloth worn as garment
sasih	moon
sawa	rice-field
selendang	ceremonial sash
subak	agricultural co-operative responsible for distribution of water
suling	flute
taman	garden
titi	bridge
tjili	symbolic representation of female form
topeng	mask, mask dance, masked performer
tugu	altar, shrine
turis	tourist
ukur	measure, size
ulun	head
wantilan	tiered pavilion
warung	stall serving drinks and snacks
wayang kulit	puppet shadow-play

Index

ACKNOWLEDGMENTS

Cover, Backcover	**Ingo Jezierski**
Photography	**Ingo Jezierski** *and*
8/9, 17T	**APA Photo Agency**
11T	**Max Lawrence (APA Photo Agency)**
12LM	**Philip Little (APA Photo Agency)**
13B	**Jean Kugler (APA Photo Agency)**
84	**Hans Höfer (APA Photo Agency)**
Handwriting	**V Barl**
Cover Design	**Klaus Geisler**
Cartography	**Berndtson & Berndtson**